T0294942

The Impact of Digital Engineering on Defense Acquisition and the Supply Chain

Insights from an Industry Survey

BRITTANY CLAYTON, OBAID YOUNOSSI, SARAH W. DENTON, HILARY REININGER, ANGELA YUN, DAVID M. ADAMSON, THAO LIZ NGUYEN, JONATHAN ROBERTS, PADMAJA VEDULA, THOMAS LIGHT, AUGUSTINE BRAVO, OLUWATIMILEHIN SOTUBO, MOHAMMAD AHMADI

Prepared for the Department of the Air Force
Approved for public release; distribution is unlimited.

RAND PROJECT AIR FORCE

For more information on this publication, visit **www.rand.org/t/RRA2333-2**.

About RAND

RAND is a research organization that develops solutions to public policy challenges to help make communities throughout the world safer and more secure, healthier and more prosperous. RAND is nonprofit, nonpartisan, and committed to the public interest. To learn more about RAND, visit www.rand.org.

Research Integrity

Our mission to help improve policy and decisionmaking through research and analysis is enabled through our core values of quality and objectivity and our unwavering commitment to the highest level of integrity and ethical behavior. To help ensure our research and analysis are rigorous, objective, and nonpartisan, we subject our research publications to a robust and exacting quality-assurance process; avoid both the appearance and reality of financial and other conflicts of interest through staff training, project screening, and a policy of mandatory disclosure; and pursue transparency in our research engagements through our commitment to the open publication of our research findings and recommendations, disclosure of the source of funding of published research, and policies to ensure intellectual independence. For more information, visit www.rand.org/about/research-integrity.

RAND's publications do not necessarily reflect the opinions of its research clients and sponsors.

Library of Congress Cataloging-in-Publication Data is available for this publication.

ISBN: 978-1-9774-1364-2

Cover: Kisha Johnson/U.S. Air Force.

About This Report

In 2018, the U.S. Air Force announced a new strategy for using digital engineering (DE) in its acquisition life cycle process. The strategy emphasizes the importance of DE in improving the efficiency, effectiveness, cost, and quality of Air Force systems and highlights the need for a common digital thread that connects all aspects of the acquisition process and life cycle management of weapon systems. To help the Department of the Air Force gain insight into the potential benefits, costs, and challenges of implementing DE, RAND researchers examined the use of DE in the acquisition life cycle.

This report summarizes the results of an industry survey that was designed to assess the progress of DE implementation and to identify implementation challenges and opportunities along with possible metrics for tracking DE implementation. It is one of a pair of reports that examine the role of DE in Air Force weapon systems acquisitions. The other report in this series is

- Brittany Clayton, Obaid Younossi, Benjamin J. Sacks, Thao Liz Nguyen, Jonathan Roberts, Thomas Light, Victoria A. Greenfield, and David M. Adamson, *The Impact of Digital Engineering on Defense Acquisition: A Look at Air Force Pathfinder Programs*, forthcoming, Not available to the general public.

The research reported here was commissioned by the Air Force Cost Analysis Agency (AFCAA) and conducted within the Resource Management Program of RAND Project AIR FORCE as part of a fiscal year 2023 project, "Assessment of Digital Engineering: Implications for Weapon System Programs and Supply Chain Adoption." This effort builds on a project documented in a separate restricted report that was also sponsored by AFCAA.[1] These closely related reports share some material, including descriptions.

Project AIR FORCE

RAND Project AIR FORCE (PAF), a division of RAND, is the Department of the Air Force's (DAF's) federally funded research and development center for studies and analyses, supporting both the United States Air Force and the United States Space Force. PAF provides the DAF with independent analyses of policy alternatives affecting the development, employment, combat readiness, and support of current and future air, space, and cyber forces. Research is conducted in four programs: Strategy and Doctrine; Force Modernization and Employment; Resource Management; and Workforce, Development, and Health. The research reported here was prepared under contract FA7014-22-D-0001.

---

[1] Thomas Light, Obaid Younossi, Brittany Clayton, N. Peter Whitehead, Jonathan P. Wong, Spencer Pfeifer, and Bonnie L. Triezenberg, *A Preliminary Assessment of Digital Engineering Implications on Weapon System Costs*, RAND Corporation, 2021, Not available to the general public.

Additional information about PAF is available on our website:
www.rand.org/paf/

This report documents work originally shared with the DAF on September 11, 2023. The draft report, dated September 2023, was reviewed by formal peer reviewers and DAF subject-matter experts.

Acknowledgments

The authors thank Ranae Woods, Director of the Air Force Cost Analysis Agency, for supporting this important work and providing helpful guidance. We appreciate Kevin Neary's assistance as our action officer throughout this effort. We are grateful to Steve Turek, technical director of the DAF's Digital Transformation Office, who took interest in this effort, provided expert knowledge, and connected us to key members of DE efforts in the defense industry. We also thank the American Institute of Aeronautics and Astronautics and the Aerospace Industries Association for helping develop and facilitate this industry survey. PAF Resource Management Program Director Stephanie Young and Associate Program Director Anna Jean Wirth provided valuable oversight, guidance, and comments throughout this effort. Finally, we thank Peter Whitehead and Alexis Lasselle Ross for their thorough reviews of the document and constructive feedback.

Summary

Issue

Digital engineering (DE), as defined by the U.S. Department of Defense (DoD), is "an integrated digital approach that uses authoritative sources of system data and models as a continuum across disciplines to support life-cycle activities from concept through disposal."[2] DoD embraced DE in its *Digital Engineering Strategy*, released in June 2018.[3] The strategy outlines the Air Force's vision for using DE to improve acquisitions and provides guidance on how to implement DE across the acquisition life cycle. The goals of the strategy are to improve the efficiency, effectiveness, and quality of Air Force systems. The use of DE is premised on the view that it can achieve these goals by improving the design, schedule, and cost of Department of the Air Force (DAF) weapon system acquisitions.

To date, there has been no empirical analysis of the extent to which DE is yielding these benefits for industry and the DAF. To close this knowledge gap, the DAF asked RAND to investigate how DE is being implemented in defense acquisition and whether it is achieving these claimed benefits.

Approach

Our team designed and administered a survey to collect data from industry stakeholders. We complemented this by conducting an open-source literature review and discussions with key experts in government. The survey provided quantitative data on industry experience with DE. The open-source literature review allowed the team to gather information from a variety of published sources, and the discussions with key experts provided valuable insights from those with direct experience in the field.

Key Findings

We focused our survey on four themes: DE goals and implementation, costs and benefits, implementation challenges, and measuring DE success. The results of the survey are outlined below.

Potential Benefits and Challenges of DE

Implementing DE entails costs, but it is also expected to lead to a variety of benefits, according to industry respondents. The major drivers of costs for implementing DE included information

---

[2] Office of the Deputy Assistant Secretary of Defense for Systems Engineering, *Digital Engineering Strategy*, U.S. Department of Defense, June 2018.

[3] Office of the Deputy Assistant Secretary of Defense for Systems Engineering, 2018.

technology (and related costs); data management and governance; and hiring, training, and retaining a qualified workforce. The largest benefits of DE are expected during the operating-and-support phase. Improvements to cost, schedule, and performance are expected to occur as a result of more-authoritative data management and decisionmaking that is informed by modeling and data analytics. Improvements in systems engineering and increases in automation are also potential benefits, along with increases in innovation during development and production. Other benefits include reduced uncertainty in operations and sustainment and a reduction in the need for physical tests. Performance-related benefits are already coming to fruition.

The main challenges in implementing DE are associated with a lack of standardization and interoperability of tools, software, and models; a shortage of skilled personnel; and a need for cultural change. These issues are reflected in the need for better tools and infrastructure and the difficulty in integrating legacy systems.

Measuring the Impact of DE

One quality that is important for leaning into the DE space is the ability to measure the impact of using DE approaches to ensure that they are working as intended. Many survey respondents were not aware of how their leadership intends to measure DE success or what metrics are being tracked. Because implementation of DE has not yet resulted in notable cost savings or schedule reduction, most benefits to date are anecdotal. Still, some qualitative benefits are being realized. These include increased complexity in system design and an expanded trade space of design options during the analysis of alternatives and Milestone A efforts. Those involved with DE activities have also observed improved collaboration and communication among stakeholders, leading to more effective decisionmaking and reduced risk.

Implications for the DAF

The insights from the survey, along with inputs from other experts and open-source literature, suggest actions that the DAF should consider when implementing DE for defense acquisition programs:

- **Develop goal-oriented plans of action.** To ensure successful implementation of DE for defense programs, it is essential to develop goal-oriented plans of action tailored to the unique characteristics and objectives of each program.
- **Manage the lack of standardization and interoperability.** Defense programs must confront the lack of standardization and interoperability among government stakeholders and industry partners. Tools, software packages, and models that vary across these entities need to be identified and effectively managed.
- **Adopt strategies for hiring and retaining skilled personnel.** The shortage of personnel with the necessary expertise in digital engineering and related fields can hinder the DAF's ability to thrive in DE environments.

- **Be mindful of the need for cultural change.** Without purposeful change management and a drastic shift in culture that is centered around collaboration, communication, and innovation, successful implementation of digital engineering within the DAF will likely not materialize.
- **Collect cost and schedule data at a low level.** Impacts from DE may not be apparent at the platform level. Therefore, programs should aim to track data at the engineering activity or system component level to use in assessing the impact of DE implementation.
- **Track qualitative benefits.** While the DAF is still collecting data on the cost and schedule impacts of digital engineering, performance-related benefits that are already being realized should be documented.
- **Investigate sustainment impacts.** DE is expected to have the most significant impact during a weapon system's sustainment phase. The DAF should investigate the transition of digital artifacts from development and production into sustainment.

Contents

Figures and Tables

Figures

Tables

Chapter 1

Introduction

The U.S. Department of Defense (DoD) policy on digital engineering (DE) is outlined in the *Digital Engineering Strategy*,[4] which was released in June 2018. The policy outlines the Air Force's vision for using DE to improve acquisitions and provides guidance on how to implement DE across the acquisition life cycle.

In its strategy document, DoD defines the term *DE* as "an integrated digital approach that uses authoritative sources of systems data and models as a continuum across disciplines to support lifecycle activities from concept through disposal."[5] DE can be seen as automated support to the systems engineering process, which is described by the Defense Acquisition University as "an interdisciplinary engineering management process that evolves and verifies an integrated, life-cycle balanced set of system solutions that satisfy customer needs."[6] Programs are now being encouraged to develop DE implementation plans at their inception.[7]

The policy emphasizes the importance of DE in improving the efficiency, effectiveness, and quality of Air Force systems and highlights the need for a common digital thread that connects all aspects of the acquisition process. The policy also emphasizes the importance of collaboration and communication among stakeholders and the need for a culture that embraces DE.[8] In addition, the policy outlines specific goals and objectives for implementing DE, such as developing a DE workforce, establishing DE standards and tools, and integrating DE into the acquisition process.

Background

This work builds on previous work performed by RAND.[9] That work arrived at the following observations:

---

[4] Office of the Deputy Assistant Secretary of Defense for Systems Engineering, *Digital Engineering Strategy*, U.S. Department of Defense, June 2018.

[5] Office of the Deputy Assistant Secretary of Defense for Systems Engineering, 2018, p. 3.

[6] Defense Acquisition University, "DAU Glossary Definition," *ACQuipedia*, undated-a.

[7] The DE implementation plan should establish "the data strategy and the data requirements to aid in developing the request for proposals (RFPs) and for executing a model-based enterprise effort"; it should also specify what government data rights are needed so that the government has access to the necessary data (U.S. Air Force, *AF Digital Enterprise Guidebook*, undated, Not available to the general public). As of June 2021, the Long Range Stand Off program was the only Air Force program identified as having a formal DE implementation plan.

[8] Thomas Light, Obaid Younossi, Brittany Clayton, N. Peter Whitehead, Jonathan P. Wong, Spencer Pfeifer, and Bonnie L. Triezenberg, *A Preliminary Assessment of Digital Engineering Implications on Weapon System Costs*, RAND Corporation, 2021, Not available to the general public.

[9] Light et al., 2021.

- **So far, programs have used tailored implementations of DE to address unique challenges to those programs.** There has not been a one-size-fits-all approach for the application of DE within defense weapon system programs, and this lack is likely to continue. It is not a panacea to be applied universally.

- **Before cost savings or other benefits from government DE efforts are realized, there will likely need to be significant investments made by DoD and/or the Department of the Air Force (DAF).** Those investments could take a variety of forms, such as investing in information technology infrastructure; in models and tools; in the development of standards for models, data, and architectures; in the securing of data rights; and in personnel with DE expertise.

- **Investments to support DE will likely affect both contractor and government program office costs.** Cost analysts should consider investments that will need to be made by both contractors and the government when developing independent cost estimates and reviewing contractor cost proposals for programs pursuing DE concepts.

- **DE could be employed for a variety of reasons beyond potential cost savings.** Different programs are likely to pursue DE for different reasons. DE could cause a program to cost more even over its life cycle, but that could be justified if it is allowing the program to achieve other objectives (such as reducing schedules or schedule risk, improving quality, and enhancing weapon system performance). In one of its most commonly cited uses, that of digital twins,[10] DE supports enterprise objectives that could allow systems to be transformed in ways that accrue benefits far beyond the original development program. Understanding why a program is pursuing DE is critical when thinking about the implications of those efforts for cost estimates.

- **Although there is plenty of anecdotal cost evidence, there are almost no verifiable data to inform cost analysis on the magnitude or likelihood of cost savings generated from DE.** As a result, cost analysts should hesitate to incorporate cost savings from DE without strong evidence presented by a program office or other stakeholders.

The previous report made several recommendations,[11] including the following:

- **Develop a repository of information for programs taking advantage of DE.** Information collected from programs should include any DE-specific requirements being pursued by programs (such as development of integrated digital environment, government reference model, digital twins, or transfer of data rights) and their costs. As programs mature, the Air Force Cost Analysis Agency and other organizations should seek to document and validate any savings from DE-related activities.

---

[10] As defined by Defense Acquisition University, *digital twins* are "a virtual replica of a physical entity that is synchronized across time. Digital twins exist to replicate configuration, performance, or history of a system" (Defense Acquisition University, "Glossary Term: Digital Twin," webpage, undated-d). A digital twin is a digital recreation of the platform, which can demonstrate performance and other features based on data from the physical platform it is replicating.

[11] Light et al., 2021.

- **Develop an evaluation process to assess DE efforts and their impact on program costs and other outcomes.** This should include the establishment of processes and protocols for tracking and evaluating DE efforts, claims, and impacts.
- **Investigate how DE efforts are affecting suppliers and supply chains.** There is concern that suppliers associated with major defense acquisition programs are not being fully integrated into DE efforts and therefore might be limiting the DE benefits of programs.
- **Study the synergy of core systems engineering practices with DE concepts.** The specific ways in which DE might support broader systems engineering goals should be analyzed, as should gaps where near-term investments could be made.

Objective and Approach

Building on the previous project, we continued to investigate the anticipated challenges and benefits of DE during weapon system acquisition. In particular, we examined how programs are implementing and tracking DE through discussions with program offices. Our project team collected information from applicable program offices, primes (that is, providers contracting directly with a government program), and open sources to explore the relationship with the supply chain. We also collected data from suppliers supporting a DE program to gain insights into their experiences and challenges. By investigating these areas, we intended to provide a more comprehensive understanding of the challenges and benefits of DE implementation and to identify potential strategies to overcome the barriers to successful implementation.

Our team used a multimethod approach over the course of the 12-month project, conducting (1) a survey designed and executed to collect defense related industry perspectives on our research questions, (2) an open-source literature review, and (3) discussions with key experts in government and industry.

This report focuses on presenting the survey results, which were complemented by the other efforts. The open-source literature review allowed us to gather information from a variety of published sources, while discussions with key experts provided valuable insights from those with direct experience in the field. Overall, the multimethod approach allowed us to develop an informed survey instrument, which we provide in Appendix A. The survey design and analysis benefited from a detailed review of related literature and discussion with industry and government on specific pathfinder programs.[12]

Literature Review

We conducted a systematic review of open-source literature to investigate the impacts of DE on defense and nondefense projects. First, we defined the scope of the review, which encompassed DE activities, costs, benefits, challenges, and metrics. Next, we performed a web scraping exercise to collect and sift through a voluminous amount of journal articles. The collected articles were then screened

---

[12] Within the context of defense acquisition, the designation of a pathfinder program is often used to test new acquisition approaches and to identify challenges, risks, or both with the new approach.

and evaluated to ensure that only relevant articles were reviewed. With the information collected, we were well suited to understand the implementation of DE in industry to frame our discussions and inform our design of the survey instrument (Appendix A). This review also helped identify potential metrics (Appendix B) for government in industry to gauge implementation of DE.

Discussions with Government and Industry

Our team conducted more than 20 discussions with more than a dozen government leaders, subject-matter experts, defense industry partners, and industry experts associated with defense and nondefense projects implementing DE. These discussions were conducted using a standard protocol and were not for attribution, meaning that comments made during the interviews would not be attributed to the person who said them. By leveraging a standard protocol and ensuring non-attribution, the team was able to gather candid feedback and insights from a variety of stakeholders, providing a more comprehensive understanding of the topic.

In addition, we attended a series of conferences and workshops dedicated to the topic of DE. These discussions and events included the 2023 American Institute of Aeronautics and Astronautics (AIAA) Science and Technology Forum and Exposition. There, our team met with AIAA's Digital Engineering Integration Team, which shared insights into how aerospace industry is progressing its DE implementation. We also attended the inaugural Digital Engineering for Defense Summit, which allowed us to gain valuable government and industry perspectives on DE implementation with defense acquisition. These discussions and events were instrumental in informing the team's observations.[13]

Limitations of the Research

The limitations of this research stem from the immaturity of programs implementing DE and a resulting lack of quantitative data because many programs are still in the early stages of their life cycle. This limits the run time of DE activities and affects realized benefits. When these programs are more mature and have progressed through production and into sustainment, we should have more (and more comprehensive) data points for comparison. Additionally, there are still varying definitions of DE, which can make it difficult to compare and evaluate different programs. Moreover, program acquisition strategy is an important determinant in deciding when and how to implement DE. For example, the option for implementing DE is more limited for a modification program than it is for a new start program.

Although the survey administered for this project proved to be a useful tool for gathering information and insights, it also has several limitations. One limitation of the survey we conducted involves its short turnaround time; the survey was only open for three weeks, which might have limited the number of responses. Another is that the results might not be fully representative of the perspectives of nonparticipants. In addition, there were variable response rates for survey questions,

---

[13] The details of our industry and government discussions are provided in the companion to this report. See Brittany Clayton, Obaid Younossi, Benjamin J. Sacks, Thao Liz Nguyen, Jonathan Roberts, Thomas Light, Victoria A. Greenfield, and David M. Adamson, *The Impact of Digital Engineering on Defense Acquisition: A Look at Air Force Pathfinder Programs*, RAND Corporation, forthcoming, Not available to the general public.

which might have affected the overall quality of the data collected. A third limitation of our survey is the subjective nature of responses. Respondents might interpret questions differently or provide responses that are influenced by personal biases or experiences. The project team could not ask follow-up questions because of participant anonymity, and this circumstance made it difficult to clarify responses or gain a deeper understanding of the data collected. Despite these limitations, the research and survey conducted for this report provide valuable insights into the implementation of DE in defense acquisition, and they highlight areas where further research and development are needed.

Organization of This Report

This report is organized into seven chapters and four appendixes. Chapter 2 characterizes the survey responders. Chapter 3 describes the DE activities that defense programs are undertaking and their associated goals. Chapter 4 outlines the costs and benefits of DE. Chapter 5 highlights challenges with implementing DE. Chapter 6 discusses metrics being collected or that could potentially be collected to track DE implementation and success. Chapter 7 summarizes our main observations. Appendix A presents the survey distributed to industry. Appendix B summarizes our literature review on DE metrics. Appendix C provides a review of the impacts that DE has had on cybersecurity.

Chapter 2

Industry Survey

The industry survey that we conducted is the primary focus of this report. The objectives of the survey were to identify the impact of DE on the supply chain and to assess the benefits and challenges the aerospace industry faces. The construction of the survey was informed by our industry and government expert discussions and by the review of relevant literature, and the survey was designed to collect data on the following areas of interest: goals of DE implementation, activities undertaken to accomplish DE, costs and benefits of DE implementation, challenges that firms are facing with implementing DE, and metrics to measure DE success. The survey design benefited from consultation with RAND subject-matter experts, U.S. Air Force Office of Air Force Cost Analysis Agency principals, and the AIAA Digital Engineering Integration Committee. The survey was distributed to more than 300 people across the aerospace industry. We collaborated with AIAA and the Aerospace Industries Association to announce the survey and invite the participation of those groups' members who were associated with DE. The 38-question survey was deployed for three weeks via a web-based platform and closed on July 28, 2023. We received a total of 69 responses, with sample size varying by question. For example, we received 69 responses to the leading demographic questions but far fewer for some of the open-ended questions. The survey consisted of a mix of question types: multiple choice, open ended, and rank order. The survey protocol is provided in Appendix A.

Although the survey population consisted largely of defense industry primes and suppliers at firms ranging in size, most respondents were from large companies with 1,000 or more employees. As shown in Figure 2.1, 80 percent of all respondents are from large firms.

Figure 2.1. Respondents' Firms' Sizes

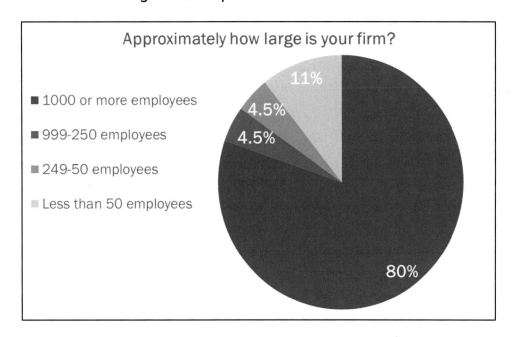

Slightly more than one-half of respondents come from companies that serve as both prime and supplier, as shown in Figure 2.2.

Figure 2.2. Respondents' Firms' Roles in Defense Contracts

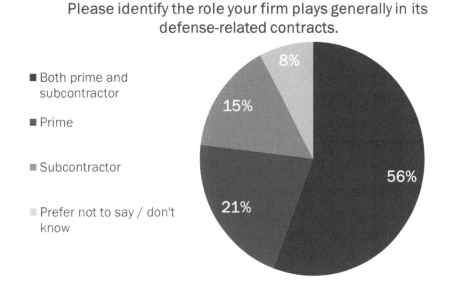

About one-half of respondents come from firms whose revenue is primarily associated with defense-related business, as shown in Figure 2.3.

Figure 2.3. Respondents' Firms' Revenue from Defense-Related Business

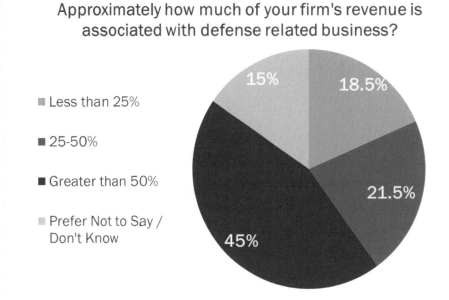

Approximately how much of your firm's revenue is associated with defense related business?

- Less than 25%
- 25-50%
- Greater than 50%
- Prefer Not to Say / Don't Know

15%
18.5%
21.5%
45%

It is important to note these demographics because they might affect how respondents answered survey questions. With the limited number of respondents, however, it is difficult for us to assess differences among firm size, prime or supplier role, or a firm's revenue source. Thus, we consider the survey responses at the total level without discriminating across demographics.

Chapter 3

Digital Engineering Goals and Activities

In this chapter, we summarize respondents' views on the goals, activities, and coordination of DE efforts. We explore why firms are implementing DE, the activities on which firms are focusing, and how firms are coordinating across stakeholders to implement DE.

Goals and Implementation

We first explored why programs are implementing DE. Our discussions with industry and government experts indicated that reasons vary depending on the goals of the stakeholders. Some goals listed were increasing quality, adhering to schedule, encouraging innovation, and containing cost. Achieving such goals requires determining which activities should be implemented. Not all DE activities can be implemented; thus, our experts noted that prioritization of tasks should also be defined by project goals. DoD and Air Force Acquisition stakeholders and industry leadership should be clear in articulating the main objectives of the program to ensure that everyone is working toward the same end. By focusing on goals and prioritizing tasks, projects can ensure that they are making the most effective use of DE and achieving the desired outcomes.

Our survey results echoed these responses. Respondents stated that their firms were actively investing in DE activities. About one-half of respondents indicated that reasons for implementing DE were similar across defense-related programs or contracts. This implies that firms are seeing a united front from defense leadership on reasons for DE implementation. Firms with fewer defense-related contracts also had similar reasons for implementing DE in the commercial sector. The top reasons that firms reported for engaging in the implementation of DE were to attain the intended system quality or performance, to contain cost, and to adhere to schedules. Respondents also stated that their firms expected to receive a lot of internal benefits from implementing DE.

One respondent voiced a caveat that industry members consider when adopting DE: Costs are higher and more uncertain in the beginning, and benefits are often delayed. Sometimes, the main reason to implement DE is contractual requirement:

> While we know the ultimate benefits are improved performance, schedule, and cost, these outcomes are not immediate reasons to implement. In these early days, performance, schedule, and cost are at higher risk. Costs to implement are often higher up front and difficult to justify to business leadership. There is still uncertainty in how to properly execute this approach, and not all solutions exist to deliver the full value proposition. While there is strong belief that performance, schedule, and cost

will ultimately be improved, the only reason driving adoption is compliance to the contract requirements.

Another respondent shared a similar observation:

> It is contract-requirement driven. Digital engineering could be beneficial for work we do in commercial industrial sectors as well, but we don't see significant adoption in those sectors without any unifying forcing function.

Additionally, there appears to be a need for a strong, unifying champion's voice to adopt DE and articulate its goals to successfully lead a DE effort. One participant observed that a strong voice and clear communication of goals are lacking:

> I've seen [DE] implementation across a range of joint service programs at the OUSD [Office of the Under Secretary of Defense] level, at my local org[anization], at some of the larger program offices, and my local division. The reasons and value proposition is all over the place, and relatively uncoordinated.

Survey respondents were aware and supportive of not only DE goals but also the clarity that comes from unified leadership and a clear statement of DE goals at the outset that can help guide the DE process for each project.

Activities

Survey results indicate that the goal enabling specific program objectives should be kept in mind when selecting DE implementation activities, and these should be activities that will generate the largest return on investment.[14] As an example, the program could create digital twins only for specific components that will inform certain decisions rather than creating a larger number of digital twins that will be underutilized.

More than one-half of the survey respondents stated that DE was changing their firm's business model. Respondents described changes in a variety of areas, such as improving efficiency and performance, modernizing technology, changing policies and procedures, and investing. Table 3.1 provides examples of business model changes.

---

[14] We explore this topic in more detail in the companion to this report; see Clayton et al., forthcoming.

Table 3.1. Business Model Changes According to Survey Responses

Business Model Change	Example Activities
Efficiency and performance	Increased coordination, merging of documentation, reduction of scrap, early emphasis on modeling, focus on first-time quality
Technology modernization	Insertion and integration of latest technologies, transition from outdated technologies
Policy and procedure changes	Focused DE initiatives, new standards to implement DE, updated contractual language, targeting training and curriculum
Investments in DE	Moving from document-based to model-based design, incorporating DE principles, software integrated into a product from design through analysis

NOTE: Responses were provided in an open-ended format.

Survey respondents indicated that their firms were engaged in a variety of DE activities. Top activities listed were curating data and models (including integrating their firm's data systems with government data systems to support real-time data), developing a digital twin for internal use, developing a digital twin for the government's use, and using model-based test and evaluation methods in place of physical test and evaluation methods.

It is critical to recognize that DE activities can look different depending on several factors, including the type of system or platform, the maturity of the system design, and the age of the system or acquisition in its life cycle. For example, DE for a major weapon system might look different from DE for a comparatively minor acquisition. DE implementation for a new system or platform might be different than it would be for a system that is being upgraded or modernized. Overall, DE implementation must be tailored to the specific needs and characteristics of each system or platform, taking into account a variety of factors to ensure that it is implemented effectively and efficiently.

Coordination and Collaboration

Overall, contributors emphasized that coordination and collaboration across all stakeholders is key to realizing DE benefits and mitigating its costs. Failure to collaborate could not only limit DE benefits but also create problems within defense acquisition. One example focused on subtier suppliers trying to adhere to different sets of demands across projects. If a subtier supplier supports multiple defense projects and each project has different requirements and deliverables for implementing DE, the supplier will struggle to manage these demands across projects. This could result in inefficiencies and rework.

We asked respondents to describe their firms' levels of coordination and collaboration in DE activities. We gathered that firms coordinate DE efforts in two ways: project-based communication and industry-level communication. *Project-based communication* refers to technical and nontechnical communication with stakeholders (customers, primes, and suppliers). Examples of project-based communication are customer "show and tell" events, collaborating in working groups, and focusing on collaboration early on. One example of project-based technical collaboration that illustrates the extent of technical collaboration in which primes engage was described by a respondent as follows:

11

We have developed a methodology for facilitating "supplier readiness" to consume model-based assets and defined the technical data package that needs to be resubmitted to design engineering. We have also established operating policies, procedures, and standard work by program. We are also attempting to coordinate collaboration on shared libraries of reference architectures and models to simplify requirements definitions, but this hasn't had significant success.

Industry-level communications refers to working as a firm with other groups or firms on nonproject work to improve DE. Examples of industry-level communications are firms working in larger organizations to align DE efforts by implementing and developing standards, sharing lessons learned, and networking with each other. Table 3.2 shows a matrix of examples for how principal stakeholders collaborate on DE.

Table 3.2. Ways That Firms Coordinate and Collaborate

Stakeholder	Project-Based Communication	Industry-Level Communication
Customers	• Developing standards • Making tools • Collaborating early	• Using customer "show and tell" • Establishing working groups
Primes and suppliers	• Developing standards • Implementing program execution	• Comparing across companies • Networking
Industry organizations	• Aligning DE efforts • Creating data standards organizations	• Making decisions about DE implementation • Setting data standards

Many respondents emphasized that stakeholders (such as primes and suppliers) must coordinate on DE activities to realize benefits. Conversely, a failure to coordinate could limit benefits and could create more challenges in acquisition as suppliers try to adhere to a variety of different requirements. Failure to coordinate could also produce a lack of standards, leading to inefficiencies. Survey respondents suggested leveraging a common ontology of consistent terminology and basic concepts that would enable coordination across the supply chain.

A clearly defined supply chain with a communicated flow of requirements from prime to subcontractor is one way to encourage coordinated implementation of DE. This ensures timely access to critical information needed for design and manufacture of parts. More than one-half of respondents said their firms obtained their requirements from the government. About one in three respondents said requirements were set internally. Finally, about one-fourth reported that requirements were conveyed by the prime contractor. Overall, participants reported that firms shared requirements when it made business sense to do so and/or was necessary.

Chapter 4

Costs and Benefits

This chapter presents analysis of survey responses regarding the costs and benefits of DE for defense acquisition. Our research revealed several costs related to the implementation of DE in defense acquisition. As shown in Figure 4.1, survey respondents identified information technology (IT) and related costs as the biggest drivers to DE implementation, notably IT infrastructure, information security, and data storage. Software, models, and tools were also identified as major costs to DE implementation. The categories of data management and governance and of hiring, training, and retaining a qualified workforce also ranked as cost drivers but were identified as slightly less prohibitive than the other categories.

Figure 4.1. Costs of Implementing Digital Engineering

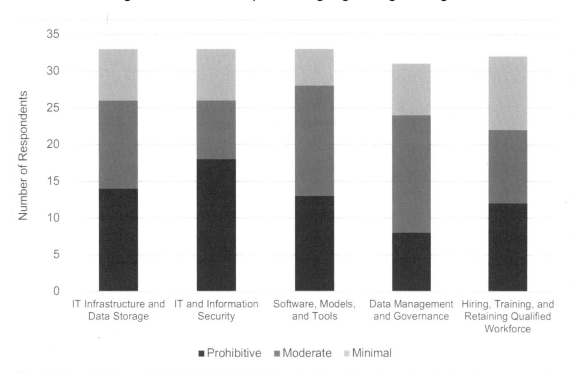

SOURCE: Features information from industry survey results.
NOTE: Responses were to a prescribed list of items.

Firms noted that without effective management practices, it is difficult to contain DE implementation costs. As one survey respondent wrote,

> Any one of these could become prohibitive without management. Only a portion of the workforce has desire to learn this new way of working, [and today] software, data

assets, and tools are low capability and struggle to support functions outside of engineering (e.g., supply bases may not be ready to consume model-based assets and don't often own all possible software packages to access the asset in the native format. "No quote" rates are extremely high, or quotes include nonrecurring engineering cost). [Moreover,] the data governance and security implications of these highly data-rich design assets [are] largely unknown today.

According to government stakeholders, there are costs related to the workforce, such as hiring, training, and retaining workers with the right skill sets for DE implementation. Government stakeholders are dedicating more money to DE-focused integrated project teams and adding DE-specific documentation to their programs in the form of strategies and plans. Another cost stems from the need for the right software packages. Obtaining these consumes both time and money. Depending on the software package that primes and suppliers are using, government program offices might need to switch from a familiar software package and retrain staff, adding to the costs of DE implementation.

Similarly, our discussions with industry stakeholders have echoed many of the comments from the government side. Hiring and training the right workforce for DE implementation is challenging, and obtaining the appropriate clearances and dealing with classification issues requires time and money.

Expected Benefits of Digital Engineering

Building on the findings from our previous study,[15] our survey results indicate that the DAF needs to implement DE across acquisition programs if it wants to leverage lessons learned, data, insights, and other benefits. Even potential enterprise investments (such as IT infrastructure and architecture; personnel recruitment and training; and software, models, and tools) need shared requirements across programs to maximize benefits from initial investments. Although the empirical basis for identifying specific benefits of DE for DAF programs remains nascent, our survey results support the notion that industry anticipates that DE will contribute to cost and schedule goals.

We first asked participants to rank how much DE is likely to contribute to cost containment and schedule goals through the life cycle of a program. Figure 4.2 shows how survey respondents estimated the level of DE contributions to cost containment and schedule goals by life-cycle phase.

---

[15] Light et al., 2021.

Figure 4.2. Contributions of Digital Engineering to Cost Containment and Schedule Goals

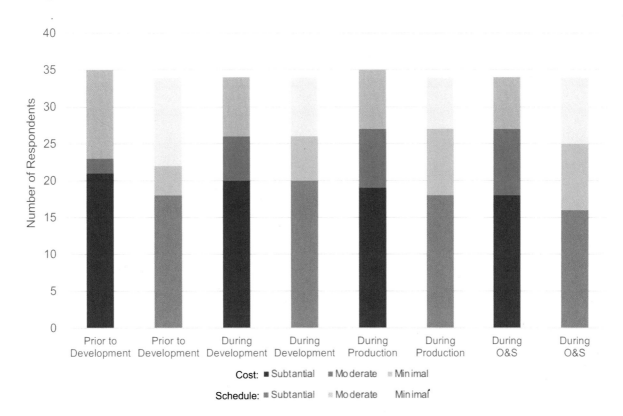

SOURCE: Features information from industry survey results.

Survey respondents specified that during development, DE contributes the same to cost and schedule goals. Overall, our industry survey indicated the following perceptions of cost:

- Around one-half of respondents said that DE substantially contributes to cost containment, and around one-third said that DE contributes substantially to schedule goals **prior to development.**
- Around one-half of respondents said that DE contributes substantially to cost containment and schedule goals **during development.**
- Around one-third of respondents said that DE contributes substantially to cost containment and schedule goals **during sustainment.**

Reported differences between DE contributions to cost and schedule are minimal. However, prior to development, industry respondents report more DE contributions to cost containment goals.

We then asked participants which benefits are most likely to be achieved. Figure 4.3 depicts the benefits resulting from DE implementation, as reported by more than 65 percent of firms responding to the industry survey.

Figure 4.3. Benefits of Implementing Digital Engineering

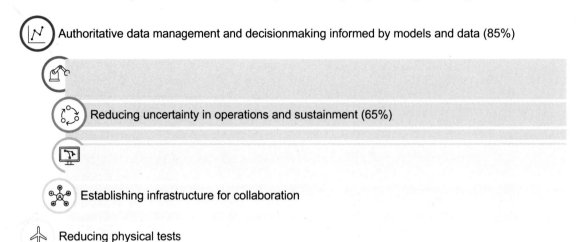

Authoritative data management and decisionmaking informed by models and data (85%)

Reducing uncertainty in operations and sustainment (65%)

Establishing infrastructure for collaboration

Reducing physical tests

SOURCE: Features information from industry survey data.
NOTE: Numbers in parentheses indicate the percentage of firms reporting that benefit. We provide percentages only for the top three responses, which yielded results of 65 percent or higher.

The greatest benefits and challenges identified were related to software, models, tools, and data, as shown in Figure 4.4. Specifically, 85 percent of industry survey respondents reported authoritative data management and decisionmaking informed by models and data as the greatest benefits of implementing DE. Most respondents reported that availability, quality, management, and interoperability of software, models, tools, and data were the greatest challenges to implementing DE.[16]

Notably, these benefits and challenges are interrelated. For example, the benefits of authoritative data management might be achieved only by overcoming data availability, quality, and management challenges. Similarly, model- and data-informed decisionmaking requires overcoming availability, quality, and interoperability challenges with software, models, and tools.

---

[16] In our results, 81 percent of respondents reported data availability, quality, and management as the greatest challenge; 69 percent of respondents reported that the greatest challenge was availability, quality, and interoperability of software, models, and tools.

16

Figure 4.4. Greatest Benefits and Challenges of Implementing Digital Engineering

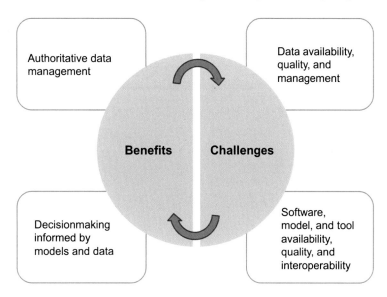

SOURCE: Features information from industry survey data.

Realized Benefits of Digital Engineering

Our discussions with government and industry suggested that many of the benefits of DE that have already been realized or achieved are not related to cost or schedule. While the acquisition community is still collecting data on the cost and schedule impacts that DE might have, performance-related benefits are already coming to fruition. Although these benefits are difficult to measure empirically, stakeholders are confident that the program is already benefiting from these aspects of DE.

One of the main benefits of DE is increased performance. DE enables more-accurate and more-comprehensive modeling and simulation of defense systems, and it can also lead to increased system complexity because it allows for better detailed and nuanced design. This increased complexity can be challenging, but it also provides opportunities for innovation and improved performance. Another benefit of DE is an expanded trade space of options during system design downselect, allowing stakeholders to explore a wider variety of options and make more-informed decisions. Finally, DE can improve communication and collaboration among stakeholders, enabling better decisionmaking and reducing the risk of errors and delays.

One discussion with a government program office indicated the impact that DE has on operator input design. Warfighters appreciate the ability to see system designs before they are delivered, allowing them to communicate preference and articulate operational challenges. The collaborative infrastructure of DE enables a tight feedback loop between operator and designer, which is highly valued. This can help resolve design issues earlier.

Chapter 5

Implementation Challenges

This chapter focuses on the challenges of implementing DE in defense acquisition experienced by all stakeholders, such as government program offices, primes, and subcontractors. Our research indicates that the challenges of DE implementation are varied, but we identified some consistent themes, notably a lack of standardization and interoperability, a shortage of skilled personnel, and the need for cultural change. The need for better tools and infrastructure, the difficulty of integrating legacy systems, and the need for better collaboration and communication among stakeholders are other challenges. By identifying these challenges and understanding their root causes, stakeholders can work together to develop solutions and overcome the barriers to successful DE implementation.

Challenges Identified with Digital Engineering Implementation

Figure 5.1 depicts the challenges resulting from DE implementation, as reported by more than 60 percent of firms in the industry survey.

Figure 5.1. Challenges of Implementing Digital Engineering

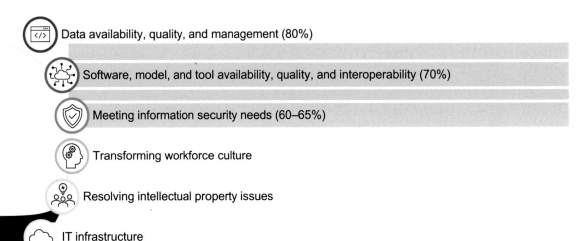

Data availability, quality, and management (80%)

Software, model, and tool availability, quality, and interoperability (70%)

Meeting information security needs (60–65%)

Transforming workforce culture

Resolving intellectual property issues

IT infrastructure

SOURCE: Features information from industry survey data.
NOTE: Numbers in parentheses indicate the percentage of firms reporting that benefit. We provide percentages only for the top three responses, which yielded results of 65 percent or higher.

One specific example indicated that setting up the environment is difficult in a variety of ways:

> Poorly performing technical infrastructure is a primary challenge to successful execution today. Configuring these environments is difficult. Not all software solutions and manufacturing standards required for this approach exist yet.

Although firms did not rank IT infrastructure as the greatest challenge, industry survey respondents connected poorly performing infrastructure to the lack of software solutions. Figure 5.2 shows how firms ranked the challenges they identified earlier in the industry survey.

Figure 5.2. Greatest Challenges Faced by Industry in Implementing Digital Engineering

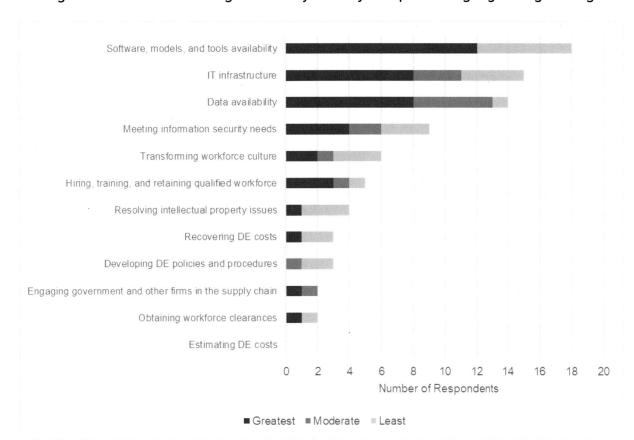

SOURCE: Features information from industry survey results.
NOTES: We asked firms to rank their top five challenges; however, some ranked all challenges while others only provide one or two rankings. For example, although no respondents ranked "estimating DE costs" as one of their top five challenges, one respondent ranked it as the eighth most challenging aspect of implementing DE. In this figure, we do not include any rankings beyond the top five. We found some discrepancies within individual survey responses between challenges identified and their associated rank order of importance.

To get a closer look at what activities are happening up and down the supply chain (and the challenges associated with them), we asked firms about tool sets used to implement DE.

Custom Tool Sets Are Employed When Prescribed Tool Sets Present Challenges

One way to organize and coordinate DE implementation across the supply chain is for the government to prescribe tool sets. However, firms pointed out problems with prescribed tool sets, highlighting issues with impeding coordination. Firms reported that interoperability posed the largest barrier to the use of prescribed tool sets, closely followed by lack of fidelity and high costs associated with creating and maintaining the necessary IT infrastructure and obtaining commercial licenses. Custom tool sets are often required to meet cost, schedule, and performance goals. For example, firms reported that prescribed tool sets

> are not interoperable. There are always differences in what is prescribed in the program and what already exists in an organization's current environment (and every other environment that organization may need to interact with). Tool providers often demonstrate sterilized examples of a "digital twin" or "digital engineering" using only their software. In reality, these are always patchwork environments that have little to no interoperability, particularly in business-to-business collaborative environments.

Firms not only reported that prescribed tool sets lack interoperability, they also highlighted how lack of interoperability in tool sets often requires additional workforce training. However, it is not clear whether these barriers are limited to prescribed commercial tool sets; custom tools might pose similar challenges. For example, custom tool sets likely lack interoperability with U.S. government IT infrastructure. Similarly, the cultural shift required of the workforce is not limited to the tool sets used. The DE process is intensive for firms and affects many areas of the firms' operations. Firms stated that government-prescribed tools prove challenging for DE:

> The current tools prescribed by the U.S. government are old and [not interoperable]. Many rely on . . . software-centric language for digital engineering . . . [which] is too difficult for the average person to learn, and the tools are not designed to work together. Thus, a tremendous amount of time is wasted trying to move data around, [which] causes configuration management difficulties.

Digital Engineering Necessitates a Cultural Shift Across the Workforce

Workforce issues pose another major challenge. Firms responding to the industry survey identified three separate workforce challenges that pose challenges to DE implementation:

- transforming the workforce culture (around 65 percent)
- hiring, training, and retaining a qualified workforce (around 55 percent)
- obtaining security clearances for their workforce (around 30 percent).

Firms indicated that only a portion of the workforce has a desire to learn and adapt to DE workflows. For example, industry survey respondents mentioned that cultural shifts are particularly challenging within the context of meeting cost and schedule goals:

Cultural shifts are always difficult and require a steady walk through the transition. [It's] always easier to do things the way you have always done them, especially when there is a schedule crunch.

As another put it,

Changing the way we work using digital engineering [is a big challenge]. You can replace tool sets, but this doesn't change the way we work. Advanced modeling and simulation development is the next step in the DE saga, but it is expensive and technologically challenging.

Classification issues were at the forefront of our discussions with government and industry, though not highlighted in our survey results. Security approvals (both security clearances for new hires and permission to transfer models or upload software packages to a classified network) do not move as quickly as desired, and classification challenges plague both government and industry. The security clearance process has been a hurdle in getting new engineers engaged with classified projects. Likewise, we heard anecdotes of delays in loading software packages onto classified networks and challenges related to gaining access to government networks. A closer look at DE's implications on cybersecurity can be found in Appendix D.

Measuring Implementation of Digital Engineering Across the Life Cycle Is Difficult

Survey respondents and discussion participants highlighted difficulties in measuring DE implementation. These challenges are often the result of several issues. Programs implementing DE have not had the runtime necessary to truly identify all costs and benefits resulting from DE implementation. Impacts span the entire life of these programs, with many lasting several decades between development and disposal. Respondents noted that larger programs struggle to track costs and benefits across a typically larger supply chain. Measuring costs across subcontractors that all use different work breakdown structures can become unmanageable.

One respondent mentioned that

Because this approach drives full life-cycle benefits, it is difficult to measure. Many of our programs are early in the digital engineering cycle. We are mostly seeing increases to real cost and only have theoretical schedule and product performance improvements.

In Chapter 6, we discuss in more detail how some of the challenges discussed in this chapter affect the ability to measure DE implementation.

Potential Metrics Reported in the Survey

This chapter summarizes survey responses related to metrics to assess costs and benefits and to support implementation. We use the term *metric* to refer to measuring current or anticipated processes, materials, workflows, or other aspects of DE to track and improve the implementation of DE benefits. Survey findings complement the metrics identified in Appendix B and suggest that DE metrics need to be standardized but are difficult to track across the full life cycle of larger programs.

Metrics to Assess the Benefits of Digital Engineering

We asked respondents to discuss what kinds of metrics their firms already use to assess the benefits of DE, but more than one-half of the respondents preferred not to say or did not know. Of those who did share metrics, scheduling metrics were cited most often. Reported scheduling metrics included such procedures as on-time product deliveries, on-time Contract Data Requirements List deliveries, hours per drawing sheet, product development cycle time reduction estimates, and milestones accomplished. Other cited metrics were the number of model-based systems engineering (MBSE) programs and financial or cost metrics (such as return on investment and earned value). Some respondents listed the size of the program as a factor in measuring DE benefits and challenges:

> Smaller programs have a lot more flexibility to capture metrics because they are generally contained, especially the classified ones. The use has proven extremely efficient when applied. Larger programs [are] a lot more difficult. Especially when partners and major suppliers are a critical part of the design and deployment of the system/platform. But where DE has been applied, we have seen substantial improvements.

Our data collection efforts made clear that programs with many parties involved, particularly in design and deployment, can make it difficult to capture metrics. Although DE can be challenging to measure for larger programs, some firms did not doubt that there have been notable improvements. However, another respondent raised considerations that offset DE benefits:

> We are measuring potential benefits to cost, schedule, and product performance but are currently seeing these benefits offset by several headwinds: (1) training engineers and designers to work in this new way, (2) limited use of these large data assets outside of engineering functions (software interoperability is poor and lightweight viewers are insufficient), (3) lack of system integration and software capability drags on performance of engineering functions, [and] (4) lack of

general infrastructure handling the implications of modeled data assets (ownership and path to revenue, authoritative conformance documentation, organizational models, collaborator/supplier relationships, etc.).

In addition to metrics, participants suggested that additional information be collected to help provide the context of the DE landscape. They mentioned wanting more details on programs beyond what is and is not being done, a consistent file or file format, more standardization across the industry on DE through a defined reference model architecture, and more collaboration with the customer and suppliers. This information would help in facilitating metrics or defining more-effective metrics.

Proposed Metrics to Assess the Benefits of Digital Engineering

More than 80 percent of participants from industry indicated that helpful metrics to assess the benefits and challenges of DE would measure cost, schedule, and performance. Cost metrics included the cost of quality, the cost for product testing and verification, and the cost of implementation. Schedule metrics involved tracking the time to first-time quality, the reduction of hours spent on functional tasks, the speed of delivery, and the speed of key segments of workflow. Lastly, performance metrics were described by respondents as the first-pass yield, defect prevention, and reducing the impact of rework on cost, schedule, and performance. These types of metrics are not surprising. They tie to the benefits that respondents expect to realize through DE, such as overall efficiency, meeting schedule, and better performance. The survey asked firms to rank their reasons to implement DE. Participants ranked intended quality or performance, cost containment, and adherence to schedule as the top reasons they were implementing DE.

Although most respondents did not know or preferred not to say what metrics their firms collected, there seemed to be an appetite for metrics among survey participants. When asked whether specific metrics would help firms assess the benefits of DE for defense contracts, the vast majority of respondents stated that the metrics would be helpful. The proposed metrics are shown in Table 6.1; the top-ranked metrics were performance improvements of technical requirements (such as mass, function, and noise), reducing physical tests, and cost reductions of changes or rework.

Table 6.1. Additional Metrics That Participants Say Would Help Their Firms Assess Benefits of Digital Engineering

Rank	Proposed Metric	Percentage
1	Physical test reduction	86
2	Performance improvement (mass, function, noise) of technical requirements	85
3	Cost reduction of changes or rework	83
4	Cycle reduction (speed) of developing products and technologies	80
5	Productivity improvement (speed) of people working	77
6	Delivery and/or schedule improvement	77
7	Part or system cost reduction	74

To collect metrics that identify a reduction in cost or schedule or an improvement in productivity, firms would need to establish a baseline for comparison purposes. For example, an estimate for physical tests would need to be calculated as a baseline (using analogous historical data or engineering judgement). This baseline would then be compared with physical tests that are required by the system as a way of identifying any reduction.

Respondents answered short-response survey questions to share the difficulty of measuring DE benefits. One participant said that measuring DE benefits poses a difficulty because doing so would have to cover the DE life cycle, and their program was only in the early stages:

> Because this approach drives full life-cycle benefits, it is difficult to measure. Many of our programs are early in the digital engineering cycle. We are mostly seeing increases to real cost and only have theoretical schedule and product performance improvements.

Another participant explained the connection between expected benefits and meaningful metrics:

> It depends on what MOE [measure of effectiveness] is related to the benefit to be achieved. Without a consistent application of benefit expectations, metrics are not meaningful except to a specific instance.

To have value, metrics need to measure benefit, be consistent, and be consistently applied. Though only a relatively small number of participants responded to this question, a few mentioned some additional metrics:

- maturity assessment
- architecture completeness
- requirements volatility
- shared metrics, predeveloped with incentives
- integrating systems engineering: requirements and development, basic system engineering methodology, system engineering change notice
- reference model or architecture defining DE to standardize the industry
- numerical control programming costs
- hours per unit for production.

Although this is not a complete list of possible metrics, we provide it here to capture some metrics requests made by industry and as a reference for possible future research.

Chapter 7

Key Findings and Implications

Our survey was designed to focus on four themes. We list our findings here, grouped by those themes.

Findings

Digital Engineering Goals and Implementation

- Firms were actively investing in DE activities. About one-half of respondents indicated that reasons for implementing DE were similar across defense-related programs or contracts.
- DE was changing business models. Respondents described changes in a variety of areas, such as efficiency and performance, modernizing technology, changing policies and procedures, and investing.
- Coordination and collaboration across all stakeholders are key to realizing the benefits and mitigating the costs of DE. A clearly defined supply chain with a communicated flow of requirements from prime to subcontractor is one way to encourage coordinated implementation of DE.

Costs and Benefits

- IT and related costs are reported to be the biggest drivers of DE implementation costs.
- Data management and governance and hiring, training, and retaining a qualified workforce also ranked as cost drivers by respondents but were identified as slightly less prohibitive than the previously mentioned categories.
- Many respondents said that DE substantially contributes to containing costs and meeting schedule goals prior to development. Most respondents said that the largest benefits of DE are expected during the sustainment phase.
- Authoritative data management and decisionmaking informed by models and data would be beneficial to cost, schedule, and performance, according to many survey respondents.
- Systems engineering improvements and increases in automation are theorized by respondents to be beneficial to cost, schedule, and performance.
- Respondents said that DE could lead to additional improvements that might be beneficial to cost, schedule, and performance. These possible improvements include reducing uncertainty in operations and sustainment, increasing innovation in development and production, developing digital infrastructure for collaboration, and reducing the need for physical tests.

Our discussions with government and industry suggested that many of the realized benefits of DE are not related to cost or schedule. While the acquisition community is still collecting data on the cost and schedule impacts that DE might have, performance-related benefits are already coming to fruition.

Implementation Challenges

A lack of standardization and interoperability, a shortage of skilled personnel, and the need for cultural change are main challenges identified by survey respondents. Other challenges are the need for better tools and infrastructure, the difficulty of integrating legacy systems, and the need for better collaboration and communication among stakeholders.

Measuring Success of Digital Engineering

Much of the industry is not aware of what leadership is tracking to measure DE success. This lack of awareness can make it difficult to develop standardized metrics for measuring DE success across the industry. Most benefits of DE are anecdotal, with firms expecting to see gains in performance, schedule, and cost. Although these benefits are promising, there is a need for approaches to measuring DE success that are more systematic and standardized. By developing and using clear and consistent metrics, stakeholders can better understand the impact of DE on defense acquisition and can identify areas for improvement.

DE is worth exploring and implementing in a structured way because it has the potential to provide a variety of benefits to defense acquisition. Despite the perceptions captured in the survey, the use of DE to date has not resulted in notable cost savings or schedule reduction, but it has benefited the Air Force in other ways. It has enabled increased complexity in system design and an expanded trade space of options during system design downselect. By supporting more-accurate and more-comprehensive modeling and simulation, DE can improve the quality and performance of defense systems. DE can also improve collaboration and communication among stakeholders, leading to more-effective decisionmaking and reduced risk. Overall, although the benefits of DE might not be immediately apparent in terms of cost savings or schedule reduction, it has the potential to provide significant long-term benefits to defense acquisition.

Implications

The DAF is still collecting data and learning about the impact of DE on defense acquisition, but our survey results, interviews with key experts, and review of open-source literature all suggest that the following actions would be prudent.

- **Address the lack of standardization and interoperability.** These measures could be improved for tools, software, and models within the programs, across contracts, and across the supply chain.

- **Increase the number of skilled personnel.** The shortage of personnel with the necessary expertise in DE and related fields can hinder the DAF's ability to thrive in DE environments.
- **Promote cultural change.** Without purposeful change management and a drastic shift in culture, successful implementation of DE within the DAF—with a focus on collaboration, communication, and innovation—is not likely to materialize.
- **Collect cost and schedule data at a low level.** Impacts from DE might not be apparent at the platform level; therefore, programs should aim to track data at the engineering activity or system component level to assess the impact of DE implementation.
- **Track qualitative benefits.** While the DAF is still collecting data on the cost and schedule impacts of DE, performance-related benefits are already being realized and should be documented.
- **Investigate sustainment impacts.** DE benefits are expected to be greatest during a weapon system's sustainment phase. The DAF should investigate the transition of digital artifacts from development and production into sustainment. Additionally, cost and schedule data should be tracked to assess impact.

Survey Instrument Distributed to Aerospace Industry

In this appendix, we reprint the survey as it was distributed to aerospace industry respondents.

Survey Instrument

This survey is a collaboration of RAND, an independent nonprofit institution, and the U.S. Air Force's Office of Air Force Cost Analysis Agency. We are surveying clients and contractors involved in digital engineering (DE) implementation to understand DE's impact on weapon system costs and the supply chain.

The survey should take 15–20 minutes and will not collect any personal or identifiable information. Your participation is entirely voluntary, and you can choose not to participate in the survey or skip any questions you do not wish to answer. All responses to this survey are anonymous— we will aggregate all survey data to ensure that your responses cannot be attributed to you, and the survey administrator will not access or report on IP [internet protocol] addresses collected passively. As such, there are few risks to the potential for connecting your response to your person and there are no other expected risks from your participation in this survey. Please do not include any classified information within your responses to this survey.

For questions about the survey, please contact Dr. Obaid Younossi at obaid@rand.org or Ms. Brittany Clayton at bclayton@rand.org.

For questions about your rights as a survey participant, you can contact RAND's Human Subjects Protection Committee at (310) 393-0411, ext. 6369 or at hspcadmin@rand.org.

1. Approximately how large is your firm?

    a. Less than 50 employees
    b. 50–249 employees
    c. 250–999 employees
    d. 1,000 or more employees
    e. Prefer not to say/don't know

2. Approximately how much of your firm's revenue is associated with defense-related business?

    a. Less than 25 percent
    b. 25–50 percent
    c. Greater than 50 percent
    d. Prefer not to say/don't know

3. With which of the following organizations does your firm currently hold contracts? (Please check all that apply)

    ☐ U.S. Army
    ☐ U.S. Air Force
    ☐ U.S. Space Force
    ☐ U.S. Navy
    ☐ U.S. Marine Corps
    ☐ Other federal agencies
    ☐ Industry/private sector
    ☐ Prefer not to say/don't know

4. What type of defense-related programs does your firm currently support? (Please check all that apply)

    ☐ Acquisition Category I (ACAT I): a Major Defense Acquisition Program (MDAP) that is estimated to require more than $525 million for RDT&E [research, development, test, and evaluation] or more than $3 billion for procurement or is designated by the Milestone Decision Authority (MDA) as a special interest program.
    ☐ Acquisition Category II (ACAT II): a major system that does not meet criteria for ACAT I and is estimated to require more than $200 million for RDT&E or more than $920 million for procurement or is designated by the MDA.
    ☐ Acquisition Category III (ACAT III): a program that does not meet the dollar value thresholds for either ACAT I or ACAT II and is not designated a major system by the MDA.
    ☐ Prefer not to say/don't know

For the following questions, please use the Department of Defense's definition of digital engineering, primes, and subcontractors:

- Digital engineering (DE) is "an integrated digital approach that uses authoritative sources of systems data and models as a continuum across disciplines to support life-cycle activities from concept through disposal."
- Primes are those providers directly contracting with the government program.
- Subcontractors are those contracting with the prime to support the government contract.

5. Please identify the role your firm plays generally in its defense-related contracts.

   a. Prime contractor
   b. Subcontractor
   c. Both prime and subcontractor
   d. Prefer not to say/don't know

6. How, if at all, has digital engineering led to your firm changing its business model (i.e., "power by the hour," "time & material," etc.)? Please briefly describe.

7. Has your firm undertaken any of the following digital engineering activities to support a defense-related program or contract? (Please check all that apply)

   a. Developing and applying a "digital twin" for the firm's own, internal use
   b. Developing and delivering a "digital twin" for the government's use
   c. Integrating your firm's data systems (e.g., containing engineering or related technical data) with government data systems to support real-time data-sharing
   d. Using model-based test and evaluation methods during development or production in place of physical test and evaluation methods
   e. Curation of data and models
   f. Prefer not to say/don't know
   g. Other, please specify one or more options

8. Please rank the following reasons for implementing digital engineering in your firm's work on defense-related programs or contracts in terms of their order of importance. (1 = greatest importance, 5 = least importance)

   ____ Cost containment
   ____ Adherence to schedule
   ____ Attainment of intended system quality or performance
   ____ Compliance with government and/or contract requirements
   ____ Other (please fill in the blank below)

9. If you ranked "Other" above, please describe it below:

10. What kinds of metrics <u>would</u> help your firm assess the benefits of digital engineering for its work on defense-related programs or contracts?

   a. Prefer not to answer/don't know
   b. Please specify:

11. In addition to those you mentioned above, would any of the following metrics also help your firm assess the benefits of digital engineering for its work on defense-related programs or contracts?
(Please check all that apply)

    a. Productivity Improvement (Speed) of People Working
    b. Cycle Reduction (Speed) of Developing Products and Technologies
    c. Performance Improvement (Mass, Function, Noise) of Technical Requirements
    d. Part or System Cost Reduction
    e. Change/ReWork Cost Reduction
    f. Physical Test Reduction
    g. Delivery/Schedule Improvement

12. What kinds of metrics does your firm already collect to assess the benefits of digital engineering for its work on defense-related programs or contracts?

    a. Prefer not to answer/don't know
    b. Please specify:

13. In addition to those you mentioned above, do any of the following metrics already help your firm assess the benefits of digital engineering for its work on defense-related programs or contracts? (Please check all that apply)

    a. Productivity Improvement (Speed) of People Working
    b. Cycle Reduction (Speed) of Developing Products and Technologies
    c. Performance Improvement (Mass, Function, Noise) of Technical Requirements
    d. Part or System Cost Reduction
    e. Change/ReWork Cost Reduction
    f. Physical Test Reduction
    g. Delivery/Schedule Improvement

14. Are the reasons your firm is implementing digital engineering:

    a. Very similar across defense-related program or contracts
    b. Sometimes similar across defense-related programs or contracts
    c. Rarely similar across defense-related programs or contracts
    d. Not applicable

15. If you would like to comment on your answer above, please use the space below.

16. Insomuch as you can compare your firm's reasons for implementing digital engineering in defense-related and commercial environments, are they:

    a. Very similar across defense-related and commercial environments
    b. Sometimes similar across defense-related and commercial environments
    c. Rarely similar across defense-related and commercial environments
    d. Not applicable

17. Please use the space below to make any comments to your answer above.

18. For your firm's defense-related programs or contracts, how much of a contribution is digital engineering likely to make to cost containment in each stage below? (on a scale of 1–5; 1 = substantial contribution, 5 = negligible contribution)

    ____ Prior to development
    ____ During development
    ____ During production
    ____ During operations and sustainment

19. For your firm's defense-related programs or contracts, how much of a contribution is digital engineering likely to make to schedule goals in each stage below? (on a scale of 1–5; 1 = substantial contribution, 5 = negligible contribution)

    ____ Prior to development
    ____ During development
    ____ During production
    ____ During operations and sustainment

20. How is digital engineering providing—or expected to provide—benefits to cost, schedule, and/or performance in your firm's work on defense-related programs or contracts? (Please check all that apply)

    a. Making authoritative data easier to locate, manage, and use
    b. Developing, integrating, and using models and data to inform decisionmaking
    c. Improving the quality or processes of systems engineering
    d. Making it possible to incorporate technological innovation in development and production
    e. Supporting more precise manufacturing, e.g., to stricter standards
    f. Reducing uncertainty and/or costs in operations and sustainment
    g. Establishing infrastructure for stakeholders to perform activities, collaborate, and communicate
    h. Increasing automation/autonomy
    i. Increasing organization agility
    j. Reducing physical test with virtual verification/validation
    k. None
    l. Other, please specify one or more options

21. Please rank the three most important ways in which digital engineering is providing—or is expected to provide—benefits to cost, schedule, and/or performance in your firm's work on defense related programs or contracts. (1 = greatest benefit)

_____ Making authoritative data easier to locate, manage, and use
_____ Developing, integrating, and using models and data to inform decisionmaking
_____ Improving the quality or processes of systems engineering
_____ Making it possible to incorporate technological innovation in development and/or production
_____ Supporting more precise manufacturing (e.g., to stricter standards)
_____ Reducing uncertainty and/or costs in operations and sustainment
_____ Establishing infrastructure for stakeholders to perform activities, collaborate, and communicate
_____ Other

22. If you selected "Other" above, please specify below.

23. How substantial are the costs to your firm of implementing digital engineering in its work on defense-related programs or contracts in each of these areas? (on a scale of 1–5; 1 = minimal cost, 5 = prohibitive cost)

_____ IT infrastructure, including data storage
_____ Software, models, and tools
_____ Data management and governance IT or information security
_____ Hiring, training, and/or retaining a qualified workforce
_____ Other

24. If you indicated "Other" above, please specify below.

25. What challenges is your firm facing—or is it expecting to face—in its implementation of digital engineering in defense related programs or contracts? (Please check all that apply)

   a. Building and/or maintaining IT infrastructure, including data storage capacity
   b. Ensuring the availability, quality, and/or integrating/interoperating of software/models/tools
   c. Ensuring the availability, quality, and/or integrating/interoperating of data (e.g., through data standards)
   d. Meeting needs for IT, data, and/or other information security
   e. Hiring, training, and/or retaining a qualified workforce
   f. Transforming the workforce culture to adopt and support digital engineering
   g. Obtaining security clearances for workforce
   h. Resolving intellectual property issues, including data rights and licensing
   i. Estimating the costs of implementing digital engineering
   j. Recovering the costs of implementing digital engineering
   k. Developing policies and procedures to guide the implementation of digital engineering
   l. Engaging with the government or other firms in the supply chain (e.g., effective communication of requirements from/to Program Managers, primes, or subcontractors, IT/software gaps between your firm and the government or with other firms, etc.)
   m. None
   n. Other

26. Please comment below with any additional information on the nature of the challenges or mitigations you indicated above.

27. Based on the selections you made in question 25, please rank the 5 biggest challenges your firm is facing—or is expecting to face—in its implementation of digital engineering:

   1)
   2)
   3)
   4)
   5)

28. If you indicated "Other" above, please specify below.

29. From whom does your firm typically obtain requirements for implementing digital engineering on defense related programs or contracts?

    a. The government (e.g., program office)
    b. The prime contractor
    c. A subcontractor
    d. Digital engineering is an internal management decision
    e. Prefer not to say/don't know
    f. Other, please specify one or more options

30. Does your firm typically convey requirements for implementing digital engineering to other firms that work on defense-related programs or contracts?

    a. Yes
    b. No

31. Please tell us your firm's rationale for either conveying or not conveying requirements for implementing digital engineering.

32. What steps is your firm taking to coordinate/collaborate its digital engineering efforts with the government and/or other firms in the supply chain?

33. Are Digital Engineering toolsets dictated or prescribed across the supply chain to be used in your current defense contracts?

    a. Yes
    b. Sometimes
    c. No

34. Based on your experience, what are the barriers to using prescribed toolsets?

35. Based on your experience, what are the benefits to using prescribed toolsets?

36. When toolsets are not prescribed, do you have custom toolsets that you use for your digital engineering efforts?

    a. Yes
    b. Sometimes
    c. No

37. If yes, why were these tools developed?

    a. Lack of fidelity of commercial tools
    b. Lack of availability of a commercial tool to meet your needs
    c. Cost of commercial tool/license
    d. Prefer not to say/don't know
    e. Not applicable
    f. Other, please specify

38. Please comment below with any addition information or elaborate on any software tool decisions you indicated above.

Thank you very much for your responses. We appreciate the time you spent on this study and your thoughtful answers.

For questions about the survey, please contact Dr. Obaid Younossi at obaid@rand.org or Ms. Brittany Clayton at bclayton@rand.org.

Digital Engineering Metrics

Introduction

This appendix highlights some of the metrics commonly recommended to assess the effectiveness of DE practices. These metrics were obtained through a literature review.

Search Strategy

We conducted our search using the keywords "Digital Engineering" and "Measure*" or "Digital Engineering" and "Metric*." We used PRIMO, which is RAND's knowledge services platform that accesses several databases, including Science Direct, Scopus, and Web of Science. This search identified 304 English-language documents, which we reviewed for their relevance to the study. A further search using the keywords "Model Based Systems Engineering" and "Measure*" or "Model Based Systems Engineering" and "Metric*" was conducted. We used this second search term of "model based systems engineering" because *DE* is a relatively new term and because model-based systems engineering is a subset of DE.[17] This search identified 417 documents. Both searches identified 583 unique papers with the keywords, but, after a review of their titles and abstracts, nine were found to be most relevant to this study. These papers are

- "Model-Based Systems Engineering: Evaluating Perceived Value, Metrics, and Evidence Through Literature"[18]
- "Towards Developing Metrics to Evaluate Digital Engineering"[19]
- "Digital Engineering Measures Correlated to Digital Engineering Lessons Learned from Systems Engineering Transformation Pilot"[20]

---

[17] *Model-based systems engineering* is "the subset of digital engineering, specifically limited to systems engineering activities and artifacts." See Kaitlin Henderson and Alejandro Salado, "Value and Benefits of Model-Based Systems Engineering (MBSE): Evidence from the Literature," *Systems Engineering*, Vol. 24, No. 1, 2021.

[18] Kelly X. Campo, Thomas Teper, Casey E. Eaton, Anna M. Shipman, Garima Bhatia, and Bryan Mesmer, "Model-Based Systems Engineering: Evaluating Perceived Value, Metrics, and Evidence Through Literature," *Systems Engineering*, Vol. 26, No. 1, 2023.

[19] Kaitlin Henderson, Tom McDermott, Eileen Van Aken, and Alejandro Salado, "Towards Developing Metrics to Evaluate Digital Engineering," *Systems Engineering*, Vol. 26, No. 1, 2023.

[20] Mark R. Blackburn, Tom McDermott, Benjamin Kruse, John Dzielski, and Tom Hagedorn, "Digital Engineering Measures Correlated to Digital Engineering Lessons Learned from Systems Engineering Transformation Pilot," *Insight*, Vol. 25, No. 1, March 2022.

- "Measurement Framework for Model-Based Systems Engineering (MBSE)"[21]
- "Value and Benefits of Model-Based Systems Engineering (MBSE): Evidence from the Literature"[22]
- *Systematic Literature Review: How Is Model-Based Systems Engineering Justified?*[23]
- *DE Metrics: Categorize the Benefits and Value of Digital Engineering*[24]
- *A Framework to Categorize the Benefits and Value of Digital Engineering*[25]
- *Investigation of Leading Indicators for Systems Engineering Effectiveness in Model-Centric Programs.*[26]

Metrics and Their Definitions

This section discusses the DE metrics identified in the literature and their definitions. The metrics are derived from two categories of literature: one that discusses the benefits of DE and one that discusses the leading indicators of engineering effectiveness. Rhodes discusses the leading indicators for engineering effectiveness;[27] the other items on our list discuss the benefits that are used to justify the effectiveness of DE practices. There are claims that DE or model-based systems engineering provides benefits, but these claims have not been substantiated with adequate objective and measurable evidence.[28] The second category of literature we used in our study attempts to derive metrics for DE performance that are based on the benefits it is said to provide.

Metrics Based on Leading Indicators

One of the research questions that Rhodes tries to answer is "how does digital engineering enable current and new leading indicators to be obtained, composed and made available to program leaders for the purpose of assessment of engineering effectiveness on model-centric programs?"[29] Of the 18 systems engineering leading indicators, the report identifies "four leading indicators that are most likely to be generated from model information":[30]

---

[21] Kaitlin Henderson, Thomas McDermott, Alejandro Salado, and Eileen Van Aken, "Measurement Framework for Model-Based Systems Engineering (MBSE)," in G. Natarajan, E. H. Ng, and P. F. Katina, eds., *Proceedings of the American Society for Engineering Management 2021 International Annual Conference*, American Society for Engineering Management, 2021.

[22] Henderson and Salado, 2021.

[23] Edward Ralph Carroll and Robert Joseph Malins, *Systematic Literature Review: How Is Model-Based Systems Engineering Justified?* Sandia National Laboratories, 2016.

[24] Tom McDermott, *DE Metrics: Categorize the Benefits and Value of Digital Engineering*, Naval Postgraduate School, 2021b.

[25] Tom McDermott, *A Framework to Categorize the Benefits and Value of Digital Engineering*, Naval Postgraduate School, 2021a.

[26] Donna Rhodes, *Investigation of Leading Indicators for Systems Engineering Effectiveness in Model-Centric Programs*, Naval Postgraduate School, 2021.

[27] Rhodes, 2021.

[28] Henderson and Salado, 2021.

[29] Rhodes, 2021, p. 3.

[30] Rhodes, 2021, p. 25.

- *Requirements trends* refers to the "rate of maturity of the system definition against the plan."[31] This indicator provides information about the "stability and completeness of system requirements that could potentially impact design, production, operational utility, or support."[32]
- *Interface trends* refers to the "interface specification closure against plan."[33] This will affect "system architecture, design, implementation and/or V&V" [verification and validation], which could affect technical, cost and schedule baselines.[34]

  The explicit and implicit requirements identified in the model-based systems engineering database are metrics that can be used to determine the requirements trends and interface trends.[35] The explicit requirements can be obtained from the data entered into the database and generated from other data.[36] The implicit requirements are obtained from the "functional and physical models developed by engineers during requirements analysis."[37]

- *Requirements validation trends* refers to the indicator that compares the progress in validating and understanding customer requirements with the original plan.[38]
- *Requirements verification trends* refers to the "progress against [the] plan in verifying [that the] design meets the specified requirements."[39]

Metrics Based on Digital Engineering Benefits

Commonly recommended metrics (Table B.1) based on the benefits that DE is believed to provide are as follows:

- *Accessibility of information* refers to the level of "access to digital data and models to more people involved in program decisions."[40]
- *Automation* refers to the "use of tools and methods that automate previously manual tasks and decisions."[41] This metric is concerned with the ability of DE tools to reduce "human input and workload" in the engineering process.[42]

---

[31] Rhodes, 2021, p. 21.

[32] Rhodes, 2021, p. 21.

[33] Rhodes, 2021, p. 21.

[34] Rhodes, 2021, p. 21.

[35] Rhodes, 2021.

[36] Rhodes, 2021.

[37] Rhodes, 2021, p. 21.

[38] Rhodes, 2021.

[39] Rhodes, 2021, p. 21.

[40] Henderson et al., 2021, p. 316.

[41] Henderson et al., 2021, p. 316.

[42] Campo et al., 2023, p. 23.

- *Communication and information-sharing* measures the "ability to transmit data and information between team members and/or stakeholders."[43]
- *Consistency* refers to the "degree of consistency and dependability present in MBSE methodology and elements."[44]
- *Cost* refers to the cost of implementing or using DE practices.[45] This metric is cited as both a drawback and a benefit of using DE practices. It is a drawback because it is expensive to implement DE.[46] However, using DE tools also reduces cost because doing so leads to identification of defects in earlier stages, reducing the cost of defect resolution or rework in later stages.
- *Defect rate or error detection* refers to the number of defects detected in the different phases of the engineering development. DE models and tools make it possible to carry out extensive simulations of the system to identify defects that would require significant resources to resolve in later stages of the development, thereby reducing risk.[47]
- *Defect resolution or rework* refers to the additional effort needed to make changes or resolve defects identified in the engineering process. It is expected that DE tools will not only make it easier to detect errors but will also reduce the level of effort and rework required to fix the defects detected, thus making it easier to make changes in the engineering process. DE is also expected to reduce the number of errors that escape from one phase of development to the next, thereby reducing the rework effort.
- *Early verification and validation capability* refers to "moving tasks into earlier development phases that would have required effort in later phases"[48] and measures the "degree to which MBSE allows for verification, certification, testing, validation, and analysis of system, data, etc."[49]
- *Effort and hours* refers to the level of effort and number of work hours required to achieve the expected outcome.
- *Integration* refers to the use of "data and models to support both the integration of information and system integration tasks."[50]
- *Model traceability* refers to the formal linking of design, requirements, test, and other elements through models.[51] Campo et al. define *traceability* as "capability of MBSE to trace course of development from origin to current status; ability to verify the history, location, or application of an item by means of documented record identification."[52]

---

[43] Campo et al., 2023, p. 126.

[44] Campo et al., 2023, p. 22.

[45] Campo et al., 2023.

[46] Campo et al., 2023.

[47] Campo et al., 2023.

[48] Henderson et al., 2021, p. 316.

[49] Campo et al., 2023, p. 127.

[50] Henderson et al., 2021.

[51] Henderson et al., 2021.

[52] Campo et al., 2023, p. 24.

- *Model views* refers to the presentation of data and models in a "language and context" that is accessible to the different users of the models.[53]
- *Reusability* refers to the ability to reuse "existing data, models, and knowledge in new development."[54] It is also defined as the "ability of MBSE to allow for the reutilization of system elements and architecture."[55]
- *Strengthened testing* refers to the use of "data and models to increase test coverage in any phase."[56]
- *Time and schedule* refers to the time it takes to complete a program that employs DE practices. A regularly mentioned benefit of applying DE is reduced time; however, some studies have also found that applying DE increases time.[57] DE increases the time it takes to model the system and is discouraged for short-term projects for which it might not yield any positive return on investment.[58] On the other hand, DE practices reduce the overall project schedule.[59] This metric will measure the overall project schedule.

---

[53] Henderson et al., 2021.

[54] Henderson et al., 2021, p. 316.

[55] Campo et al., 2023, p. 24.

[56] Henderson et al., 2021, p. 316.

[57] Campo et al., 2023.

[58] Campo et al., 2023, p. 18.

[59] Campo et al., 2023.

Table B.1. Suggested Metrics from DE Literature

Metric	Potential Measures	DE Activity
Accessibility of information	Percentage of automated artifacts, percentage of workforce with access to model, number of single source of truth (SSOT) consumers	Model integration, product life-cycle management (PLM), data and model management
Automation	Ratio of automated to manual activities, percentage of automated artifacts or model elements, product automation, deployment lead time, number of defects detected by the model, percentage of architecting tasks automated	Digital artifacts and models, PLM, digital twinning, system architecting, automation
Communication and Information-sharing	Accessibility and availability of collaborative modeling environments, percentage of automated artifacts and model elements, percentage of workforce with access to model, readability of design information	Engineering workflows, collaborative environments, artifact synchronization, model interoperability
Consistency	Functional correctness, availability of an SSOT, cumulative changes, cumulative rework effort, error rate, percentage of standardized models, functional architecture completeness, percentage of architecting tasks automated	Requirements management, model data management, three-dimensional (3D) manufacturing, PLM
Cost	Cost-effectiveness, cost overrun, cost savings, cost avoidance because of reduced rework, cost to correct defects, return on investment, development cost, procurement cost, operating cost, benefit-to-cost ratio	Zero-cost prototyping and system implementation, automation
Defect rate or error detection	Number of errors discovered in each program phase; total number of defects found; defect density; percentage of defects discovered in the simulation stage; historical anomalies detected; defect, error, and failure rate; number of change requests; functional correctness; requirements volatility	Computer-aided design, computational fluid dynamics, finite element analysis, modeling, simulation, testing, 3D printing
Defect resolution or rework	Number of errors that escape from one phase to the next, cumulative cost of correcting defects over the life-cycle or cumulative rework effort, defect density, total number of defects, number of change requests, functional correctness, requirements volatility, defect resolution, amount of effort to discover and resolve a defect	Computer-aided design, computational fluid dynamics, finite element analysis, modeling, simulation, testing, 3D printing
Early verification and validation capability	Percentage of testing done in the models, percentage of requirements verified through automation, cumulative changes, cumulative rework effort, deployment lead time	Simulation and testing, design verification, virtual certification
Effort and hours	Number of work hours, number of systems engineering full-time equivalents, amount of effort to discover and resolve a defect, requirements volatility, number of system engineering hours per requirement	Design, modeling, simulation, testing, stakeholder requirement management

Metric	Potential Measures	DE Activity
Integration	Cumulative rework effort, functional correctness, defects discovered during integration, total interface defects	Simulation, testing
Model traceability	Percentage of elements that are fully digitally traceable, availability of an SSOT, percentage of artifacts or model elements that are automated and/or traceable, functional architecture completeness and volatility, functional correctness, product size	System architecting, data management, requirements engineering, modeling
Model views	Number of systems modeled versus the total number of systems, functional correctness, functional architecture completeness, percentage of automated artifacts or models, percentage of digitizable tasks done within model, percentage of workforce with access to model, number of SSOT consumers	Digital artifacts or models, PLM, stakeholder requirement management, system architecting, model integration
Reusability	Percentage of standardized models, ease of future modification	Digital modeling, (future) modification, standardization, modularization
Strengthened testing	Percentage of testing done in the models, deployment lead time, rework effort in physical system, total interface defects	Simulation and testing, design verification, virtual certification
Time and schedule	Number of work hours, schedule performance, response time, deployment lead time, schedule overrun, queued time, cycle time, deploy time, near-optimal time for manufacture, percentage of on-time deliveries, percentage of architecting tasks automated, amount of effort to discover and resolve a defect	3D modelling, simulation, testing, collaborative environments, model plan

Cybersecurity Implications

DoD's *Digital Engineering Strategy* outlines five strategic goals for "the use of digital representations of systems and components and the use of digital artifacts as a technical means of communication across a diverse set of stakeholders."[60] These goals are meant to give directions to the acquisition and procurement of national defense systems and, at the strategic level, to broadly inform the implementation goals of various firms and of the government (as discussed in Chapter 2). Goal Four specifies the need to "establish a supporting infrastructure and environments to perform activities, collaborate, and communicate across stakeholders." Along with an IT infrastructure that encompasses processes, methods, tools, and people, the goal incorporates the establishment of "collaborative trusted systems" that enforce protection of intellectual property, improved information sharing, and enhanced cybersecurity.[61] The National Defense Authorization Act for Fiscal Year 2022 requires the Air Force to report on the service's ability to expand DE capabilities and on the plans to "securely and effectively interchange data with operating locations to enable the local implementation of advanced manufacturing and sustainment operations."[62]

Although DE literature does mention cybersecurity of the infrastructure, cybersecurity of the supply chain, and embedded security in digital models and artifacts as an integral part of the DE transformation process,[63] the two fields have, to a large extent, developed separately for manufacturing—both for the defense industries and for commercial manufacturing. Design and development of multifaceted systems, such as weapon systems, involve development of separate models for different disciplines and engineering fields—including cybersecurity—that together enable the development of the system in question.

There is a need for a convergence of various fields necessary to support DE to ensure the security of future weapon systems. This would include prioritization of cybersecurity—to support the overall digital transformation process and environment, as well as to be embedded within the digital modeling for the security of the weapon systems. DE initiatives today are integrating data and interconnected models from various disciplines with varying levels of success, as summarized in the survey results in the previous chapters and illustrated in the companion to this report.[64] A framework for a digital

---

[60] Office of the Deputy Assistant Secretary of Defense for Systems Engineering, 2018.

[61] Office of the Deputy Assistant Secretary of Defense for Systems Engineering, 2018.

[62] Public Law 117-81, National Defense Authorization Act for Fiscal Year 2022, December 27, 2021.

[63] There are several schools of thought about the intersection of cybersecurity, information security, data and intellectual property protection, and access control. For this report and appendix, we use the term *cybersecurity* to refer to all the aforementioned disciplines.

[64] Clayton et al., forthcoming.

representation of a system is required, as is a digital thread for managing digital assets.[65] This framework can then be used to administer and govern these interconnected models across various disciplines, organizations, cultures, acquisition entities, and cyber-physical boundaries "as a continuum throughout the development and life of a system."[66] Cybersecurity would have to be the cornerstone of such a framework both for the protection of the digital thread and for the protection of the end product, the weapon system.

We have identified three areas of cybersecurity implications for DE: infrastructure cybersecurity and compliance, embedded cybersecurity for digital models and digital twins, and cybersecurity of the DE supply chain. The following sections discuss these three areas. We also discuss other implications of DE on cybersecurity, such as the benefits of DE and digital twins.

Infrastructure Cybersecurity

The DE ecosystem requirements as defined by DoD specify an infrastructure support for high-performance data analysis and computing power; secure connections; extensibility with interoperability to both unclassified and classified defense networks, industry, academia, and networks outside the continental United States; and support for software, tools, and engineering life-cycle activities.[67] For many primes and small and medium enterprises, this would require an overhaul of infrastructural support for digital asset security. The security provisioning required for supporting the DE infrastructure involves adequate and controlled access to authoritative data and information for government, industry, and other stakeholders; appropriate authentication and authorization; access for authorized users to digital models and privileges for their modification; and cybersecurity for securing proprietary information and compliance with applicable information assurance and risk management framework requirements.[68] To meet DE goals of reducing time and costs from start to completion or delivery and to improve the quality of the end products, the DE infrastructure would have to support the secure access to the "right information [at the] right time [and in the] right format"[69] to all stakeholders based on their access authorizations, thus protecting intellectual property information and enabling network security and cybersecurity.

DoD has several existing and evolving standards, doctrines and policies, and certifications to allow firms to be compliant with the latest cybersecurity infrastructure requirements. The most notable of these are the National Institute of Standards and Technology (NIST) Special Publication 800-171

---

[65] Defense Acquisition University, "Glossary Term: Digital System Model," webpage, undated-b; Defense Acquisition University, "Glossary Term: Digital Thread," webpage, undated-c.

[66] Office of the Under Secretary of Defense for Research and Engineering, Department of Defense, Mission Engineering Guide, Version 2.0, October 1, 2023; Heidi L. Davidz and Douglas W. Orellana, "Controlling the Digital Engineering Ecosystem: An Elastic Model Governance Guide for the Digital Thread," *32nd Annual INCOSE International Symposium Proceedings*, 2022., pp. 1188–1202.

[67] Office of the Under Secretary of Defense for Research and Engineering, "Digital Engineering Ecosystem General Requirements," August 3, 2021.

[68] Office of the Under Secretary of Defense for Research and Engineering, 2021.

[69] Aerospace Industries Association, *Evolving Defense Acquisition Through Digital Transformation*, August 2018.

and DoD's Cybersecurity Maturity Model Certification program (CMMC).[70] NIST's standards are the cybersecurity standards used by DoD and the federal agencies and could be considered the gold standard for cybersecurity. CMMC, which is set to be released as CMMC 2.0, provides five maturity certification levels (which are being streamlined to three in the new release) to guide defense acquisition contractors to plan their processes, milestones, and actions for a certification. On a broad scale, such certifications are necessary for ensuring consistent infrastructural and supply chain (as will be discussed in the next section) cybersecurity standards across all stakeholders on a digital thread. However, CMMC certification could create barriers of entry to small and medium enterprises that might not have the bandwidth to align with requirements in terms of processes and preparation. The costs related to obtaining such a certification, mostly in terms of implementing the required processes, might also become a barrier for entry.[71] These caveats notwithstanding, DoD and all DE stakeholders would have to enhance cybersecurity implementations to enable the consistent security of digital assets within each stakeholder's domain.

From the survey (Chapters 3 and 4), we can determine that both primes and small and medium enterprises are facing various challenges in upgrading their infrastructure to support the cybersecurity needs of DE. Among the challenges stated by survey respondents were "[intellectual property and] data-rights issues between parties, especially when working in an [integrated development environment]"; "historical (non-agile) approval processes. Legacy IT infrastructure. Non-agile funding model (Customer funding cycles)"; "requirements generally not clear on what to convey—limited incentives for doing it internally due to difficult to recover costs. [Intellectual property and] licensing concerns make negotiations complex." The survey emphasizes the challenge of supporting DE cybersecurity with infrastructure without incurring significant upfront costs to upgrade "poorly performing technical infrastructure," configuration of environments, and investing in supporting software and hardware solutions. As one respondent mentioned, the software solutions and manufacturing standards required for DE and IT infrastructure and security might not even exist yet.

Embedded Cybersecurity—Digital Model or Digital Twin

One of the main aspects of implementing DE is to ensure that cybersecurity and compliance are embedded within the weapon system or the end product—that is, engineering cyber resilient weapon systems. This is sometimes referred to as enabling cybersecurity design of the cyber-physical system or the weapon system to *shift left*.[72] This would enable determination of design issues; measurement of cyber resiliency issues; and management of data ownership and protection, classification, and

---

[70] National Institute of Standards and Technology, "Protecting Controlled Unclassified Information in Nonfederal Systems and Organizations," Special Publication 800-171, Rev. 2, February 2020, updated January 28, 2021; Chief Information Office, U.S. Department of Defense, "CMMC Model," webpage, undated.

[71] DoD also could face a dearth of qualified personnel to review, inspect, and certify firms as compliant with CMMC. See Capital Factory, "Removing Barriers to Entry for Practical Applications of Digital Engineering and Startup Collaboration," *Medium*, April 9, 2021.

[72] Office of the Deputy Director for Engineering and Office of the Under Secretary of Defense for Research and Engineering, *Engineering of Defense Systems Guidebook*, U.S. Department of Defense, February 2022.

cybersecurity of the weapon system.[73] MBSE for DE would include the cybersecurity requirements for a system along with other requirements for a model, such as parametric information, functional and nonfunctional requirements, and behavioral requirements. Hecht and Chen propose a model requirements catalog that would include cybersecurity modeling along with other nonfunctional attributes, such as reliability modeling and performance modeling.[74] The concept of digital twinning allows (1) embedding cybersecurity design patterns and modeling and (2) measuring cybersecurity to build cyber resilience end products. This can be achieved by implementing development, security, and operations (DevSecOps) approaches for digital artifacts and model development for frequent testing, detection of defects, and rapid design changes, including those related to system resilience.[75]

Securing the Supply Chain

The supply chain, which encompasses the digital thread, would be the most vulnerable part of a DE ecosystem. The establishment of digital threads would expose various entities and stakeholders in DE ecosystems to new security threats. Subtiered firms often struggle with limited resources and capability to obtain robust cybersecurity infrastructure. Data and blueprints of weapon systems would be accessible as digital assets to a large number of stakeholders, thereby creating a larger threat landscape than siloed units of responsibility and physical assets. Securing the supply chain and the digital thread would require several aspects to come together in an integrated stakeholder effort to formalize requirements and policies, including protection of cloud-based assets; access control, including zero-trust implementations; and protection of intellectual property. DoD released an action plan, developed in response to Executive Order 14017,[76] for securing defense-critical supply chains that recognizes cybersecurity and industrial security as some of the key enablers of national security. The report emphasizes the focus on cybersecurity and supply chain risk management for supply chain cyber resilience. DE supply chain security requires a more nuanced approach to the implementation of risk management and risk mitigation strategies.

Our survey respondents recognized the challenges of creating a secure ecosystem while providing access to all stakeholders. One respondent stated this challenge of collaboration between public and private organizations as

> similar in that establishing validated and authoritative models to accelerate delivery of
> capabilities is the chief priority. They are different in that defense programs are
> federally funded, and capabilities are delivered through an integrated collaboration of

---

[73] American Institute of Aeronautics and Astronautics Digital Engineering Integration Team, *Digital Twin: Definition and Value*, American Institute of Aeronautics and Astronautics and Aerospace Industries Association, December 2020; Alfred Schenker, Tyler Smith, and William Nichols, *Digital Engineering Effectiveness*, Carnegie Mellon University Software Engineering Institute and Adventium Labs, 2022.

[74] Myron Hecht and Jaron Chen, "Verification and Validation of SysML Models," *INCOSE International Symposium*, Vol. 31, No. 1, 2021.

[75] Office of the Deputy Director for Engineering and Office of the Under Secretary of Defense for Research and Engineering, 2022; David James Shephard and Julia Scherb, "What Is Digital Engineering and How Is It Related to DevSecOps?" Carnegie Mellon University Software Engineering Institute, November 16, 2020.

[76] DoD, *Securing Defense-Critical Supply Chains: An Action Plan Developed in Response to President Biden's Executive Order 14017*, February 2023; Executive Order 14017, "America's Supply Chains," Executive Office of the President, February 24, 2021.

public and private organizations, so the DE implementation has to span the program (i.e., all the collaborators). In commercial environments, most of those controls and considerations exist wholly inside the private commercial organization.

Some lessons learned from the DoD Sentinel program could provide insight into a successful incorporation of cybersecurity into DE. The Sentinel program is well known for building industry-leading cybersecurity into its system and digitally transforming its weapon system toward DE. The DoD report *Cybersecurity for DoD Acquisition Program Execution* describes best practices drawn from the Sentinel program.[77] This program found success in cyber hardening early in the program with support from resources outside the program, such as the Cyber Resiliency Office, federally funded research and development centers, and university-affiliated research center laboratories. The program developed internal cybersecurity requirements more robust than requested by formalized policies and implemented departmental structural changes to better organize cybersecurity leadership and build relevant departments. Lastly, the program implemented cybersecurity, by design, through routine red team exercises and application of system-theoretic process analysis for security.

Other Implications

Other implications of DE cybersecurity would be the adoption of DE and related workforce or personnel requirements and skill sets. The Office of the Under Secretary of Defense for Research and Engineering has created the *DE Body of Knowledge* (DEBoK) to support the DoD engineering community in the use of DE and MBSE.[78] *DEBoK* provides resources on systems engineering, software engineering, modeling, and cyber-resilient weapon systems; it also offers access to doctrine and policies, best practices, the community of practitioners, and training.[79] In addition to these efforts on upskilling the workforce, it is important for DoD and the services—including the Air Force—to assess workforce requirements in terms of additional personnel for reviewing models and design; understanding ownership and security of digital artifacts; and reviewing, assessing, and certifying various stakeholders to meet DoD cybersecurity standards.

Investments and Challenges Related to Digital Engineering Cybersecurity

As described in Chapters 3 and 4, the survey results from the industry provide insight into the status of transforming the cybersecurity implementation processes, standards, and environments. As one survey respondent exemplifies the transformation required for implementing DE practices,

> DE is transforming our company across the board. We are heavily investing in this transition to move from document-based to model-based design, development, production, services. [There are] many advantages to this, including, but not limited

---

[77] DoD, *Cybersecurity for DoD Acquisition Program Execution: Best Practices for the Major Capability Acquisition Pathway: Insights from the Ground Based Strategic Deterrence (GBSD) Program*, March 17, 2022.

[78] Thomas W. Simms, *Status of Adoption and Implementation of Digital Engineering Infrastructure and Workforce Development Within the Department of Defense*, U.S. House of Representatives Report 117-118, October 1, 2022.

[79] DoD, "CRWS-BoK," database, undated.

to efficient access to authoritative information, automated config management, [and] automated design to manufacturing model/data linkages.

As mentioned in the infrastructure and supply chain cybersecurity sections, the DE programs need to establish validated and authoritative models and their access, review, validation, and reuse at every phase of the program across the entire DoD program's integrated ecosystem while providing protection of data, datalinks, intellectual property, and the models. Responding to questions on challenges and costs to firms related to implementing DE for IT infrastructure; IT or information security; and software, models, and tools (all of which are directly related to security of the infrastructure, the supply chain, and the digital assets, including the weapon system DE models), many survey respondents specified that meeting information security needs is an existing and moderately high challenge to realizing the full implementation of DE. A majority of respondents also specified that costs for implementing IT and information security range from moderate to prohibitive, and this area is the biggest driver of costs in DE implementation. In many ways, this can be interpreted as information security, cybersecurity, data, and intellectual property protection. Visibility and access control are among the most-significant requirements of the shift to digital assets and digital threads; not only does DE create a significant infrastructural and supply chain threat possibility, it also practically makes a weapon system's blueprint into a digitized asset to be shared across various stakeholders.

But the survey also revealed that cybersecurity is still a secondary priority for firms implementing DE, the first being "establishing validated and authoritative models to accelerate delivery of capabilities." Ideally, as stated earlier, both would be prioritized and developed as an integrated engineering transformation effort. As an example, our survey of the cybersecurity cost data for a couple of programs revealed little distinction in costs at the program and infrastructure levels, the supply chain level (protection of digital thread), and embedded model cybersecurity. Most of the security-related costs are in the system engineering cycle and are significantly lower that would be expected for cybersecurity (including IT and information security) of a DE transformation. The dichotomy of the recognition of the importance, the challenges, and the potential costs of cybersecurity implementation for DE and the actual costs expended for cybersecurity reveals that there is no consistent effort tied to integrating it into, and implementing it as a part of, the DE.[80] We have to caveat this; we do not have access to all the cost data related to cybersecurity, nor do we have insight into the difference between program or infrastructure costs for DE cybersecurity and MBSE costs for DE cybersecurity.

Conclusion

As illustrated in this appendix, cybersecurity (including information, intellectual property, and data security) forms a critical aspect of successful DE implementations for DoD and the DAF. Our research found several challenges in this space. However, for a more detailed analysis of the challenges

---

[80] As stated in the accompanying RAND report on Air Force Pathfinder Programs, some programs (such as the Long Range Stand Off program) are modeling cybersecurity attack paths and entry points and reliability model testing; see Clayton et al., forthcoming. At the time of this writing (June 2023), the program was not saving much on costs, but it was gaining clarity of the process and identifying issues earlier.

of security in a DE ecosystem, a focused future study might be required. Another aspect that must be included in that analysis is the expected benefits of DE and digital twins for the cybersecurity of weapon systems. Digital twins can provide the necessary anomaly-detection mechanisms to mitigate any potential cyberthreats to the physical weapon system. The concept of *digital ghost*, for example, uses the digital twin of the physical asset as the knowledge base of the underlying system to monitor the system for anomalous behavior, the point of attack, and even methods to neutralize the effects for continued functioning of the system.[81] Therefore, the benefits of, threats from, and implications of DE on cybersecurity require deeper research in future studies.

---

[81] American Institute of Aeronautics and Astronautics Digital Engineering Integration Committee, *Digital Twin: Reference Model, Realizations & Recommendations*, white paper, January 2023.

Abbreviations

3D	three-dimensional
AIAA	American Institute of Aeronautics and Astronautics
DAF	Department of the Air Force
DE	digital engineering
DoD	U.S. Department of Defense
IT	information technology
MBSE	model-based systems engineering
PLM	product life-cycle management
SSOT	single source of truth

References

Aerospace Industries Association, *Evolving Defense Acquisition Through Digital Transformation*, August 2018.

American Institute of Aeronautics and Astronautics Digital Engineering Integration Committee, *Digital Twin: Reference Model, Realizations & Recommendations*, white paper, January 2023.

American Institute of Aeronautics and Astronautics Digital Engineering Integration Team, *Digital Twin: Definition and Value*, American Institute of Aeronautics and Astronautics and Aerospace Industries Association, December 2020.

Blackburn, Mark R., Tom McDermott, Benjamin Kruse, John Dzielski, and Tom Hagedorn, "Digital Engineering Measures Correlated to Digital Engineering Lessons Learned from Systems Engineering Transformation Pilot," *Insight*, Vol. 25, No. 1, March 2022.

Campo, Kelly X., Thomas Teper, Casey E. Eaton, Anna M. Shipman, Garima Bhatia, and Bryan Mesmer, "Model-Based Systems Engineering: Evaluating Perceived Value, Metrics, and Evidence Through Literature," *Systems Engineering*, Vol. 26, No. 1, 2023.

Capital Factory, "Removing Barriers to Entry for Practical Applications of Digital Engineering and Startup Collaboration," *Medium*, April 9, 2021. As of September 17, 2023:
https://capitalfactory.medium.com/removing-barriers-to-entry-for-practical-applications-of-digital-engineering-and-startup-46855487f177

Carroll, Edward Ralph, and Robert Joseph Malins, *Systematic Literature Review: How Is Model-Based Systems Engineering Justified?* Sandia National Laboratories, 2016.

Chief Information Office, U.S. Department of Defense, "CMMC Model," webpage, undated. As of September 17, 2023:
https://dodcio.defense.gov/CMMC/Model/

Clayton, Brittany, Obaid Younossi, Benjamin J. Sacks, Thao Liz Nguyen, Jonathan Roberts, Thomas Light, Victoria A. Greenfield, and David M. Adamson, *The Impact of Digital Engineering on Defense Acquisition: A Look at Air Force Pathfinder Programs*, RAND Corporation, forthcoming, Not available to the general public.

Davidz, Heidi L., and Douglas W. Orellana, "Controlling the Digital Engineering Ecosystem: An Elastic Model Governance Guide for the Digital Thread," *32nd Annual INCOSE International Symposium Proceedings*, 2022.

Defense Acquisition University, "DAU Glossary Definition," ACQuipedia, undated-a. As of May 10, 2024:
https://www.dau.edu/acquipedia-article/systems-engineering-process

Defense Acquisition University, "Glossary Term: Digital System Model," webpage, undated-b. As of May 10, 2024:
https://www.dau.edu/glossary/digital-system-model

Defense Acquisition University, "Glossary Term: Digital Thread," webpage, undated-c. As of May 10, 2024: https://www.dau.edu/glossary/digital-thread

Defense Acquisition University, "Glossary Term: Digital Twin," webpage, undated-d. As of May 10, 2024: https://www.dau.edu/glossary/digital-twin

DoD—*See* U.S. Department of Defense.

Executive Order 14017, "America's Supply Chains," Executive Office of the President, February 24, 2021.

Hecht, Myron, and Jaron Chen, "Verification and Validation of SysML Models," *INCOSE International Symposium*, Vol. 31, No. 1, 2021.

Henderson, Kaitlin, Thomas McDermott, Alejandro Salado, and Eileen Van Aken, "Measurement Framework for Model-Based Systems Engineering (MBSE)," in G. Natarajan, E. H. Ng, and P. F. Katina, eds., *Proceedings of the American Society for Engineering Management 2021 International Annual Conference*, American Society for Engineering Management, 2021.

Henderson, Kaitlin, Tom McDermott, Eileen Van Aken, and Alejandro Salado, "Towards Developing Metrics to Evaluate Digital Engineering," *Systems Engineering*, Vol. 26, No. 1, 2023.

Henderson, Kaitlin, and Alejandro Salado, "Value and Benefits of Model-Based Systems Engineering (MBSE): Evidence from the Literature," *Systems Engineering*, Vol. 24, No. 1, 2021.

Light, Thomas, Obaid Younossi, Brittany Clayton, N. Peter Whitehead, Jonathan P. Wong, Spencer Pfeifer, and Bonnie L. Triezenberg, *A Preliminary Assessment of Digital Engineering Implications on Weapon System Costs*, RAND Corporation, 2021, Not available to the general public.

McDermott, Tom, *A Framework to Categorize the Benefits and Value of Digital Engineering*, Naval Postgraduate School, 2021a.

McDermott, Tom, *DE Metrics: Categorize the Benefits and Value of Digital Engineering*, Naval Postgraduate School, 2021b.

National Institute of Standards and Technology, "Protecting Controlled Unclassified Information in Nonfederal Systems and Organizations," Special Publication 800-171, Rev. 2, February 2020, updated January 28, 2021. As of September 17, 2023: https://csrc.nist.gov/pubs/sp/800/171/r2/upd1/final

Office of the Deputy Assistant Secretary of Defense for Systems Engineering, *Digital Engineering Strategy*, U.S. Department of Defense, June 2018.

Office of the Deputy Director for Engineering and Office of the Under Secretary of Defense for Research and Engineering, *Engineering of Defense Systems Guidebook*, U.S. Department of Defense, February 2022.

Office of the Under Secretary of Defense for Research and Engineering, "Digital Engineering Ecosystem General Requirements," August 3, 2021.

Office of the Under Secretary of Defense for Research and Engineering, Department of Defense, *Mission Engineering Guide*, Version 2.0, October 1, 2023.

Rhodes, Donna, *Investigation of Leading Indicators for Systems Engineering Effectiveness in Model-Centric Programs*, Naval Postgraduate School, 2021.

Schenker, Alfred, Tyler Smith, and William Nichols, *Digital Engineering Effectiveness*, Carnegie Mellon University Software Engineering Institute and Adventium Labs, 2022.

Shephard, David James, and Julia Scherb, "What Is Digital Engineering and How Is It Related to DevSecOps?" Carnegie Mellon University Software Engineering Institute, November 16, 2020.

Simms, Thomas W., *Status of Adoption and Implementation of Digital Engineering Infrastructure and Workforce Development Within the Department of Defense*, U.S. House of Representatives Report 117-118, October 1, 2022.

U.S. Air Force, *AF Digital Enterprise Guidebook*, undated, Not available to the general public.

U.S. Department of Defense, "CRWS-BoK," database, undated. As of September 17, 2023: https://www.crws-bok.org

U.S. Department of Defense, *Cybersecurity for DoD Acquisition Program Execution: Best Practices for the Major Capability Acquisition Pathway: Insights from the Ground Based Strategic Deterrence (GBSD) Program*, March 17, 2022.

U.S. Department of Defense, *Securing Defense-Critical Supply Chains: An Action Plan Developed in Response to President Biden's Executive Order 14017*, February 2023.